saving face

HOW TO LIE, FAKE, AND MANEUVER YOUR WAY
OUT OF LIFE'S MOST AWKWARD SITUATIONS

andy robin and gregg kavet
illustrated by mike pisiak

SIMON SPOTLIGHT ENTERTAINMENT
New York London Toronto Sydney

SIMON SPOTLIGHT ENTERTAINMENT
An imprint of Simon & Schuster
1230 Avenue of the Americas, New York, New York 10020
Text copyright © 2005 by Andy Robin and Gregg Kavet
Illustrations copyright © 2005 by Mike Pisiak
Designed by Joel Avirom and Jason Snyder
All rights reserved, including the right of reproduction in whole or
in part in any form.
SIMON SPOTLIGHT ENTERTAINMENT and related logo are
trademarks of Simon & Schuster, Inc.
Manufactured in the United States of America
First Edition 10 9 8 7 6 5 4 3 2 1
Library of Congress Control Number 2004022100
ISBN 0-689-87890-7

contents

the workplace:

SALVAGING YOUR DIGNITY FROM NINE TO FIVE 65

sex:

GETTING TO YES, YES, YESSSS! 89

friends and family:

KEEPING YOUR WORST FROM THOSE WHO KNOW YOU BEST 105

6 what's a body to do?

PRIVATE FUNCTIONS IN A PUBLIC WORLD 143

7 clash of civilizations:

STAYING ON THE GOOD SIDE OF 6.3 BILLION PEOPLE 163

acknowledgments

We'd like to thank Tricia Boczkowski of Simon Spotlight Entertainment for conceiving the project, our editor, Patrick Price, for making it better, and all those who rescued us from awkward situations before we learned to do it ourselves: Lindsay, Anna, Roxane, Peter, Jackson, and Kirsten Larson.

AWKWARDNESS, LIKE PORNOGRAPHY, is hard to define but easy to spot: the cold sweat, the brain freeze, the sensation of having the eyes of the world upon you.

Ask anyone to tell you his ten worst experiences. A great loss or a couple of bouts of sickness or pain may be in the mix, but odds are that seven or eight are simply cringeworthy, horribly awkward moments.

We go through life trying to flee from such situations. But we fail, again and again. We get stuck, don't know what to do, and end up saying or doing things that make the encounter that much worse.

The problem is we haven't been educated. No one has systematically studied embarrassing moments and offered remedies that are easy to use.

Until now.

We have personally tested thousands of potential remedies for awkward situations. Most have failed terribly. We've been slapped, sued, screamed at, and ostracized. We've lost jobs, become estranged from our families, and severely cramped our sex lives. All for you, gentle reader.

But a few have worked. In the following pages, we tell you exactly how to extricate yourself from a wide range of sticky situations: How to greet someone when you've forgotten their name. How to dodge responsibility when you clog your in-laws' toilet. How to ask your handyman if he's stolen from you. How to dump your workplace paramour. How to return your neighbor's Weedwhacker after you've fried the motor.

So, ubiquitous as awkward situations are, you no longer have an excuse to hide in your home like some clean-shaven Ted Kaczynski. Go out, socialize, work, live, lust, and love. But keep this book handy. Because you never know when events might turn . . . well . . . awkward.

introduction:

THE TOOLBOX

THE TACTICS IN THIS BOOK work for anyone, from the brain damaged simpleton to the self-indulgent genius. However, all readers will be helped by mastering a few techniques and assembling them into what we call, collectively, "The Toolbox."

the toolbox

LYING

Make lying your friend. You will use lies, big and small, again and again. Practice your lies. Make them believable. The only thing worse than not lying at all is lying unconvincingly.

MODERN TELECOMMUNICATIONS EQUIPMENT

Because the telephone obviates face-to-face confrontation, it will be used heartily throughout this book. But to effectively maximize its power, you should also enlist a range of modern technological enhancements, including an answering machine or voice mail system, caller ID, call forwarding, call waiting, selective line blocking, and the versatile "STAR 69." Take the time to learn the limits of your particular system. How many messages does it take to fill your voice mail box? What's the code to make your phone number untraceable? Where are the dead spots in your cell phone service so you can experience convenient disconnections?

A DISTRACTED LOOK

Make it your default expression. A distracted look helps excuse a host of inconsiderate or criminally stupid behaviors. Look in the mirror and practice the look. Pick a thought to help you: Your mom just died. You're a week behind schedule on a big project. You have a deadly disease. These situations cause exactly the sort of inner turmoil that makes irresponsible actions seem inconsequential.

POVERTY

Money is a nice thing. For our purposes, poverty is better. Or at least the appearance of poverty. By pleading poverty, you can cheap-out services, lay off housekeepers and handymen, skimp on gifts, and cancel plans. For credibility, habitually complain about recent extraordinary expenses: You lost a lawsuit. Your kid needs platelet therapy. Your car fell into a sinkhole. You have to dig out, redesign, and replace the foundation on your house.

SCAPEGOATS

Nothing relieves you of responsibility faster than having someone else to blame: a secretary, an assistant, a wife, a husband. They don't have to be real; they just have to be at fault. Lay the groundwork early on by complaining about your scapegoat: "I have the worst secretary in the world. I really need to get a new secretary. You wouldn't happen to know a good secretary, would you?" For more extreme cases, consider concocting an identical twin.

Assemble your toolbox. Keep it organized, clean, and ready. You're going to need it.

1 unhappy hour:

SURVIVING PARTIES AND OTHER GET-TOGETHERS

IT IS ONLY FITTING that this book begin with an examination of the party, a premeditated series of bizarre rituals designed to disorient and embarrass the attendees through a barbaric weeding out of social rejects. There are myriad unwritten rules concerning arrivals and departures, greetings and good-byes, gifts, food, conversation, and appearance. Screw up even a little and the other participants will turn on you with withering scorn, crushing your ego and sending painful waves of embarrassment through your shattered psyche.

Only by mastering the following advice can you hope to survive the party. Learn the rules, practice the tricks, and visualize your escapes—now—before your moment of truth late one holiday night, many months from now.

1. arriving overdressed/underdressed

The average person spends five minutes a day wondering what to wear. When you're heading to a party, that period expands to five hours. Sometimes invitations offer guidance, but it's usually vague or misleading. *Festive attire* says, "There's a party. Wear clothes." *Dressy casual* means, "Dress like a schizophrenic." *Creative black tie* is the least helpful of all. Are you going to a Republican fund-raiser or a gay pride parade?

No matter what guidance you get, odds are you'll shoot high or low. You'll look either stuffy and arrogant or boorish and grubby. The only question is how to explain yourself.

TACTICS

■ where you came from

Tell people you came straight from work. If overdressed, you're a high-powered executive. If underdressed, you're a creative type: a musician, a sculptor, Richard Branson, etc.

■ where you're going

If people know the truth about where you work, talk instead about your next destination: a pool party, a debutante ball, a scavenger hunt, or the Grammys. If you're in black tie and others aren't, excitedly say you'll be performing some magic tricks later.

■ medical necessity

Blame your health: "My doctor says I have a sclerotic jugular. He told me if I wear a tie, my blood will be on his hands. Literally." If dressed too formally try, "My Achilles tendon is so frayed, these heels are the only thing keeping my foot attached to my leg. And this gown is the only thing I own that goes with them."

■ make converts

If dressed too casually, call other people "stiffs" and urge them to "loosen up." Yell, "Come on! It's a party." Spill stuff on jackets. Push people into pools. Playfully remove ties and wrap one around your head like a samurai band.

2. arriving without a gift

As you pull into the driveway of your friend's house, the balloons tied to the mailbox are the first sign this is something more than an informal get-together. Confirming your fears, every other guest seems to be carrying something: a colorful box, a decorative bag, a bottle. You look like an idiot, a bad friend, and a cheapskate.

TACTICS

■ **the glom-on**

Approach a group that has collectively purchased a generous present and ask if you can join them. Chances are they'll be happy to dilute their outlays. Make sure to sign the card with a big, bold signature and repeatedly mention the gift to your host.

If there are many group gifts to choose from, look for one that matches your own interests and talents. For example, if you're a big baseball fan, glom on to the ball game tickets. Your host will likely

assume you were the originator of the gift rather than the parasitic leech you really are.

■ the associated gift

If no group is willing to bail you out, or if the group gift is more than you care to spend, consider the associated gift. This ersatz present seems to connect with a group gift but has the advantage of not needing to be bestowed at the present time. For example, if a few others have chipped in for a tennis racket, write up a note presenting your host with a free tennis lesson. This move imparts your gift with the aura of planning and forethought, even though it contains nothing of the sort.

secret santa

Remember, it's not Santa. It's Secret Santa. All you need is to show up with something, *anything*, and you're likely to get something decent in return. Wrap up some old magazines. Stuff a box with Salada tea bags. Grab a knit cap from the lost and found. Be sure to share in the room's collective disgust when someone opens your present. Offer up your own hypothesis as to the identity of the bad Santa.

■ what's in your pockets?

A nice pen? A pocketknife? A slightly used wallet? A cool key chain? If you're wearing a new sweater or sweatshirt, remove it, steal a gift box from the present table, and presto: You're the paragon of thoughtfulness.

potluck dinner

If there's a decent restaurant or market nearby, you might grab a last minute contribution to a potluck. But what if there isn't? What if your only resource is a 7-Eleven or a snack machine? The key is to associate your crap with something better. If someone took the time to make stew, encircle the tureen with pieces of bread. Co-opt the string beans by adding a crunchy topping of crumbled Doritos. Stick chunks of Heath Bar in the ice cream. If someone asks what you brought, point to the general vicinity of the item you've co-opted and modestly say, "It came out better than I thought."

DESPERATE MEASURES

Write a short, somber note stating that a donation has been made in the recipient's name to an imaginary charity. Make it tragic, like Children's Cirrhosis Relief or Save the Puppies. Avoid answering questions by getting choked up when queried.

3. deciding whether to hug, kiss, or shake hands

You're invited to a party at the home of a couple you know. As the door opens and the hostess greets you, you start to panic: *Do we shake hands, hug, or kiss? She seems the effusive type, but I don't know her very well.*

Drained of confidence, you go in for a reluctant hug that catches her attempted handshake mid-thrust and traps it between your torsos. You disengage abruptly, your half-assed gesture looking spastic and perverted.

TACTICS

■ quarantine

This tactic is the gold standard for avoiding the smooches of the foul-breathed, slobbery, or lipstick-ridden. However, it also works beautifully for transforming potentially awkward greetings into neutral waves of the hand.

As others approach, place a hand in front of your face and regretfully say, "I don't want to give you my cold." If they don't hit the brakes, fire off a few warning coughs or blow your nose vigorously into a miniscule scrap of shredded tissue. If still undeterred, they may need to be reminded of your recent visit to the Guangdong bird market or the Kinshasa free-range monkey lab.

■ lead, don't follow

To avoid a game of greetings chicken, telegraph your move well ahead of time. After picking your poison, make it known to the recipient via outstretched arms, puckered lips, or a heartily extended hand. If time or space threaten to obscure the message, announce your intentions verbally: "I'm going to give you a big kiss!" or "Put 'er there, pardner. Let's feel that grip!"

■ group dynamics

If there are lots of people to greet, consider doing it en masse. Get everyone's attention with an extroverted, "Hey, everybody!" Then, centering your attention on faces well beyond striking distance, wave and toss out a few representative names: "Dave! Good to see you! How you doing, Sam? Mary! Susie! Joey! Look at this! Everybody's here! This is awesome! Yay!"

■ **heat of battle**

If possible, busy yourself with important tasks that occupy your hands: grilling, cooking, pouring drinks, soothing a screaming kid. . . . This busywork permits you to greet everyone with a simple smile. What's more, they'll quickly move on before you ask them to help.

cool guy handshake

Sometimes problems arise even when both parties decide to shake hands. There are many varieties of handshakes, the most problematic of which are multi-part, finger-waggling, palm-sliding whackoffs that are nearly impossible to master unless you buy or sell large quantities of illegal drugs. If you suspect you're dealing with a "cool guy," avoid embarrassment and tangled digits by coming in early and enthusiastically with an extended fist that demands to be met by another fist. Capping the punch off with a guttural "Yeah!" will signal that there's no need for further finger-waggling, pinky-snapping, or other annoying games of handsie.

4. forgetting a name

You walk into a room filled with friends and greet them one at a time: "Hi, Grace. Hey, Terence. What's up, Ted?" And then your eyes light on . . . that guy. The short guy with the thick eyebrows and a touch of eczema. . . . You worked with him for eight years. He has all those cats. Damn. You should definitely know his name.

TACTICS

■ go generic

Use babe, bud, kid, pal, tiger, friend, lady, big guy, or Miss Thang. The key here is credibility. Gain it by conspicuously using generics on people whose names you obviously know, like your wife or boss. If no one like that is around, get a running start of babes, buds, and pals before greeting the mystery person. "Tiger" will suddenly seem like the affectionate endearment it isn't.

■ **get physical**

Compensate for the lack of a mental connection by touching, patting, hugging, shaking, kissing, or mock-fighting.

■ **intimacy**

Even the vaguest memories of shared experiences, if expressed in cherished, heartfelt tones, can provide cover. Talk about that wonderful fishing trip. Ask after those adorable little felines. Even better, divulge personal details from your own life: a grandmother on lithium, a nephew marrying outside the religion, the unsettling dark splotches on your recent esophageal scan. If possible, use the sentence, "You are one of the most important people in my life right now."

■ information, please

Swap e-mail addresses, compare driver's license photos, share childhood nicknames, or ask how the person's parents came up with his or her name. If you are able to suss out the name, wait a bit before using it. Then use it, loudly and with confidence.

mispronouncing names

A frustrating variant because you *almost* know the name and want to get the credit you deserve. Sometimes your ignorance is of the length of a vowel or the stress of a syllable, as with Alicia and Andrea. If mumbling an approximation seems risky, try concocting a nickname from a portion of the name you can pronounce. For example, substitute "Sri-Man" for "Srivastava" or "A-lady" for "Alicia." Also consider using the last name only. (In some cases, this isn't practical—such as with Srivastava Megawasarthawy.)

erroneous "nice to meet you"

Implying that your previous encounters with someone didn't trigger so much as a single neuron in your brain can cause offense. Avoid the problem by using "Nice to see you" instead of "Nice to meet you" whenever greeting people—even if you think it's the first time. If you've already blurted out "Nice to meet you" and notice blood draining from the face of the person you've offended, try to recover by adding the word "here" to the end of the sentence, as in, "Nice to meet you . . . here." This suggests you've met before but never at this location. Bolster the recovery by explaining what makes the location special, such as "Nice to meet you here . . . at a party where we can finally relax and chat" or "Nice to meet you here . . . at an industrial park where we can see how America really works."

■ the mcguffin

Tell the person there's someone nearby whose name you can't remember. Ask if they wouldn't mind introducing themselves to that person to help you out. When they introduce *themselves*, make sure to listen in. This pseudo-favor also helps win points on the intimacy front.

5. mislabeling people

Pregnancy is such a miraculous, life-affirming experience that even busy strangers are tempted to take time to acknowledge it. Well-meaning questions like "Is it your first?" will usually elicit a reciprocal smile and a cheery—if well-trodden—response.

Unless, of course, the interrogator has mistaken fat for a fetus.

Let us remind you: A fetus is a source of pride and a living symbol of maternal love. Fat, or adipose tissue, is a source of shame and, in quantities large enough to be mistaken for pregnancy, a symbol of late-night ice-cream binges and unused gym memberships.

The lesson? Never label people before they have labeled themselves. An old man holding a teenager's hand might not be her grandfather. A stocky, short-haired truck loader might piss sitting down and ask her boyfriend to clean your clock if you suggest otherwise. Two willowy men holding hands might be brothers, conjoined twins, or Italians.

Of course, if the damage has already been done, you might try one of the following.

TACTICS

■ the student of mankind

After sensing your gaffe, change your tone to a blend of annoyance and sympathy, and rhetorically add, "How many times have you heard that?" while shaking your head disgustedly. You suddenly go from perpetrator to frank confidant, a student of mankind. Stick around and chat for a while. Remember: When you're a student of mankind, the world is your lesson book.

■ red herring

Blame your mistake on some extraneous clue, refusing to acknowledge the obvious one. With a mistaken pregnancy, for example, you might explain, "I saw you walking toward that baby store." After confusing a paramour for a grandfather, add, "After all, the two of you have the same facial structure." When mistaking a long-haired male clerk for a woman, say, "How do you like that? A man working at an auto parts store."

6. pretending to understand something you don't

It can happen in an instant. While chatting with someone, you let your eyes drift to the hottie across the room. Suddenly you're lost in a conversation about a movie you haven't seen, a book you haven't read, or someone named Alex who might be male or female or, conceivably, canine. You can't admit your ignorance now. You've been nodding along for five minutes. But sooner or later there might be a question you can't answer with a simple nod, mumble, or "I couldn't agree more."

TACTICS

■ **fudge it**

Cross your fingers and continue to nod, mumble, and speak in generalities. Most people don't care about your opinion. They want to hear themselves talk.

take it up a notch

No matter what the subject, it didn't materialize out of thin air. Explain you misunderstood what he was talking about, but avoid humiliation by indicating that you thought he was referring to an even more eso-teric subject: "Oh, you were talking about the *movie*. I thought you were referring to the play it was based on." If he was discussing a play, talk about the German short story that inspired it. If it's a German short story, talk about the mating traditions of the Neanderthals that served as the basis for the legend.

get offended

Pick a statement the person makes, no matter how innocuous, and turn on it. Take great offense and storm off. Not only are you out of the conversation, but you clearly possess so much knowledge of the sub-ject you won't even talk to ignorant boobs about it.

trump card

Think of something off the subject that simply must be mentioned. Try shouting, "My god, we've forgotten about the meteor shower!" or "Did you just feel that earthquake?" or "Have you seen Arnold's gift? It looks like something he found in his pocket."

7. drinking with alcoholics

It's Friday afternoon. The only thing on your mind is getting to your friend's party and pouring enough booze down your gullet to obliterate any memory of that idiot Riley's damned promotion. But halfway through your first drink, the guy you're chatting with mentions he's a recovering alcoholic. You pause mid sip. He says that your drinking is no problem, but you don't believe him. And you don't want to be the cold, insensitive bastard who picked him up and tossed him off the wagon.

TACTICS

■ the decoy

Offer to get him a ginger ale and secretly get yourself something that *looks* like ginger ale. (Scotch and soda—as well as rum, vodka, or gin mixed with ginger ale or a speck of cola—will give you the innocuous fizzy amber you're looking for.) If questioned about the slight mismatch, say they ran out of Canada Dry and gave you the cheapie store-brand.

▪ the hidden source

Go to the bar. Get a beer, and pour it into a glass. Also get a bottle of nonalcoholic beer but pour most of it in the trash. Carry both glass and bottle back to the table. As you swig down your beer, make a great show of topping it off with the remaining drops from the nonalcoholic bottle. If you repeat this process too many times to fake sobriety, blame it on the 0.5 percent alcohol they keep in "near beer" to maintain that "great beer taste."

▪ the distraction

Point out the most inebriated guy at the party. Sadly say you've seen him that way a lot. Ask if there's anything your recovering friend can do to pull him on to the wagon. After he's out of sight, jump off and rejoin the party.

8. getting caught telling tales

At a party, getting the most attention doesn't necessarily mean being the best looking or wealthiest. It means telling the best stories. In search of the spotlight, you might be tempted to embellish by adding a few harmless details here or there. You might even tempt fate by making someone else's story your own. But fate doesn't like to be tempted. What do you do when you suddenly realize the story you're telling happened to one of the very people you're regaling?

TACTICS

■ flares and chaff

Like an F-16 chased by a heat-seeking SAM, toss out misleading details and plot twists to keep the aggrieved party from zeroing in on your transgression. For example, if you're talking about catching the home run ball in game seven of the World Series, end by saying, "And then . . . then it wasn't a home run. It just looked like a home run from where I was sitting. But later, the same batter actually did hit a home run. And some guy caught it, can you believe that? Crappy luck, I guess."

■ embrace the coincidence

If your story is more one in a thousand than one in a million, you might complete your tale and let the real subject cry foul. Interrupt him, saying, "I know—it happened to you, too. Why do you think I'm telling this story? Because it's an amazing damn coincidence." You might win credibility points by pointing out a couple of minor differences in your narratives: "Of course, my guy had a leather cap. And he was working security for the Stones, not just a roadie."

■ bright lights, big city

Steal a trick from gimmicky novelist Bret Easton Ellis, who made "you" the subject of his best-selling comedy. When you see the real subject of your story in the audience, morph your first-person narrative into second. "The ball was heading right toward me. I was right under it . . . and you caught it! What a catch you made! You caught a World Series home run ball!"

When asked about your curiously inconsistent subject, explain that you've been experimenting with narrative forms and hope they've enjoyed it. Offer to tell them another story in the pluperfect tense. Alternatively, if English is not your native language, admit you sensed something was wrong and curse your crappy ESL instructor with a foreign expletive.

9. not liking the food

There's a lot of pride wrapped up in cooking. It's a personal expression of talent, effort, and cultural panache. And, of course, it's a sign of self-esteem so low it obligates you and other guests to physically bolster it with enthusiastic chewing and appreciative nods.

But just because your hardworking aunt slaved over a hot stove doesn't mean the meal's edible. Maybe she's a bad cook. Maybe she's served something you can't stand. Maybe the expiration date smudged. Whatever the case, you're in the soup. People are staring at you, and that heap of uneaten crap in front of you that isn't going away.

TACTICS

■ **napkin**

This is an option if the meal has only one or two abominable components, such as a fetid meatball or rancid peas. Dispose of the offending items by spitting into a napkin while pretending to wipe your mouth.

Paper napkins may be thrown away or flushed down toilets. Cloth napkins should be briskly but discreetly unfurled over trash cans or under-the-table "neutral zones" and inspected afterward for telltale remnants. If you're outdoors, the world is your napkin.

■ go for seconds

. . . and put stuff back. Works great with stews, stir fry, and beef stroganoff. Here's how to do it: First, talk up the meal while pushing things around a lot so it looks like you're making headway. If possible, actually ingest something inoffensive but bulky, such as French bread or mashed potatoes. After a few minutes, announce loudly that the food is so good you're going for seconds . . . but insist on serving yourself. At the serving counter, return the junk and load up on something new. If nothing's appetizing, don't worry—you went for seconds. You're in the bonus round. Nobody cares if you can't finish.

■ clean up

Like stealing a base, this tactic depends on a quick first step. Push back your chair, grab your neighbor's plate, and place it atop yours, covering the move by saying, "I'm going to do the dishes, and there's no ifs, ands, or buts about it!" A plate of equal size can easily conceal several pounds of uneaten biomatter. Do not remove it until you're alone by a garbage receptacle or disposal and can send the hidden cargo to its rightful destination.

■ shawshank redemption

In the classic movie *The Shawshank Redemption,* Tim Robbins scatters bits of prison wall around the inmates' yard to disguise his tunneling work. Borrow a trick from ol' Tim and wander around with your plate, surreptitiously crumbling the meal and scattering it around for the vermin to refuse.

■ break the species barrier

Dogs will generally eat anything, as will parrots if the pieces fit through the bars of their cages. Remember, however, that cats are carnivores and will loudly expel such foodstuffs as spinach pie in close proximity to the feeding zone. If outdoors, keep in mind that wild animals are almost always starving. Rats, squirrels, raccoons, and field mice would be happy to take your rejects in an attempt to live long enough to create another generation of starving progeny.

■ doggy bag

Make your cell phone ring and express disgust at being called away from such a fine culinary event. To assuage the host, demand a doggy bag and stuff it with oversize helpings of every dish. Make sure to call later and say how wonderful everything was, even reheated. And remember: Don't discard the bag in the host's curbside trash can.

eating other food

Sometimes you fully expect a party to have awful food or you envision long hours of small talk and cocktails before anything substantive is served. You might be tempted to make a pre-party, fast-food pit stop. Be careful. Don't park in front of the establishment, especially if it's close to your destination. The host might run out for more ice and spot your act of betrayal. And avoid the drive-through. You may be unable to ditch incriminating Styrofoam clamshells and paper bags before your arrival. Finally, consider breath mints and handiwipes. The inimitable smell of french fries will drive the starving masses at the party so wild with envy they might rat you out.

DESPERATE MEASURES

Claim an allergy. This works best when you want to avoid a particular dish, such as braised scallops, cream of tomato soup, or chicken with peanuts. Lay the issue to rest by describing in graphic detail the symptoms that would erupt were you to eat the tempting, tantalizing, wonderful-smelling items at hand. If all the dishes look terrible, you might be able to claim that the presence of one allergen taints the entire meal. Rub your neck, clear your throat, wheeze, feign tachycardia, and apologize that you weren't clearer about your dietary restrictions. Or chalk up your reticence to moral issues, refusing to be a party to the systematic murder and exploitation of animals and vegetables (making you a vegan in the former case and a crazy person in the latter). A variant is the religious exemption. Jews, Muslims, and those still finding their way can refer to obscure passages in Leviticus or Koranic rules of Haram to eliminate virtually any offensive dish. In addition, most religions incorporate days of fasting that may be utilized to skip out on particularly unholy repasts.

10. leaving early

You're not having fun. Or you've got somewhere better to go. Either way, you want to ditch this loser scene for brighter highways. Trouble is, it's "early"—that indefinable time during which your departure will cause the hostess to choke on her mini quesadilla and glumly intone guilt-provoking unanswerables like, "But we haven't had dessert . . ." or "But we need you for Parcheesi . . ." or "But we haven't watched the anniversary video. . . ."

TACTICS

■ **the fog of the party**

Look around and try to take in the overall breadth of the party, paying close attention to the level of music, the number of guests, the prevalence of self-organizing social clusters, and the general degree of inebriation. Factoring in all these accounts, is it conceivable that one could get "lost" in the "fog" of the party? Put another way, is it possible that,

despite a good faith effort, a reasonable person might fail to find the host to offer thanks and say good-bye? If so, stand near the door, wait until others aren't looking, and slip out.

■ i'll be back

When Arnold Schwarzenegger delivered his signature line to a stunned precinct captain in *The Terminator*, he put an end to all further questioning of his unusual, robotic behavior. That's because, whether Arnold knew it or not, he was exploiting a trapdoor in the human mind. "I'll be back" buys the speaker that rarest of all commodities:

time. When someone hears "I'll be back," they think, "We don't have to get into this right now. We'll deal with this later."

Trust in the power of "I'll be back." Use the phrase to get out the door, and don't worry about explaining where you're going or how long you'll be. Just walk away, secure in the knowledge you now have a day or two to think of a good excuse for your failure to return.

■ divide and conquer

If more than one person is hosting the party, there's an unwritten rule that you are permitted to thank only one before leaving. Exploit this rule by carefully choosing the host least likely to resent your early departure. This might be a host you don't know very well, a painfully shy host, or a host preoccupied with food, entertainment, or screaming kids.

endgame

Even if you have no desire to leave early, you need to properly time your exit. You don't want to be the last person at a party, the only ear for a (by now) drunk and strangely frank hostess. Moreover, her references to "that huge pile of dishes" can leave you between the Scylla of guilt and the Charybdis of dishpan hands. As the party winds down, keep track of the number of guests remaining. Work backward. A good rule of thumb is to leave no later than third to last. That way, an unexpected rush for the exits is unlikely to leave you stranded.

An advanced variation is to say good-bye to neither host and call both separately the following day. Tell Jim, "I had a chance to say good-bye to Carol, but I didn't say good-bye to you." Tell Carol, "I thanked Jim, but I had such a great time that I wanted to thank you, too."

■ habituation

Wait for guests less savvy than yourself to initiate their good-byes while keeping a watchful eye on your hostess. As soon as her pleading and disappointment fade into reluctant acceptance, jump in and say that you, too, must take your leave. Desensitized to boorishness, she will lack the energy to try to guilt you into staying.

IT SHOULD BE APPARENT NOW that parties are just no fun. But they're as good as it's going to get, considering where we're going next.

2 the service industry:

KEEPING SPIT OUT OF YOUR SANDWICH

WHETHER YOU LIKE TO ADMIT IT or not, you are a boss. You may be a peon at work, but to your hairdresser, your housekeeper, and your gardener, you're the Big Burrito. El Jefe. Generalissimo Numero Uno. And even if your staff doesn't speak Spanish, you're still pretty important. After all, it's you who makes the calls, signs the checks, and does the hiring and firing.

With power comes responsibility. And with responsibility comes awkwardness. Do you tip an usher? Do you send back an over-mayoed sandwich? Do you fire a locksmith who looks like he just escaped from Leavenworth?

It's lonely at the top. You're going to need all the friendly advice you can get. So study up.

1. dealing with someone who seems to have stolen from you

Your kitchen's being retiled and your leather jacket is missing. Do you bring it up with the workers? Do you bring it up with their manager? Do you bring it up at all?

There's a lot at risk. People don't like to be accused of stealing, especially if they didn't do it. They might get sloppy with the tiles. Or play hooky. Or pad the bill. On the other hand, it was a nice jacket. Your wealthy sister knew somebody at Ralph Lauren. Retail, that thing would've cost nine hundred, easy.

TACTICS

■ **my mistake**

Remove any intimation of blame by making the theft of the jacket somehow your fault. Slump your shoulders and sheepishly say, "I did something stupid, and I feel just awful about it. I put my jacket near where you guys had your tools. I know, I know—it was a really dumb thing to do. I realize it's a pain for you to track down the jacket and bring it back, but if you do, I promise it won't happen again."

■ **the crazy dude**

Rather than confront the workers, confide in them. Tell them you're scared. You borrowed a jacket from this crazy dude, and you seem to have misplaced it. And now the dude's going crazy! Tell them the dude is a psycho with a black belt and nothing but time and money on his hands, and he's making this whole jacket thing his number one priority: "He says if I don't find it, he'll get litigious or violent. He's so whacked he might even come after *you guys* just because you were around when I lost it."

DESPERATE MEASURES

Steal a small but expensive item from your workers' toolbox, like a carbide blade or laser level. When you notice them searching for it, tell them you're not surprised, adding, "A lot of things have gone missing here lately. Like . . . my jacket." If they don't respond, try, "Wait—I think I remember it dropping into one of the pockets of that jacket. Maybe when we find my jacket, we'll find . . . your tool."

2. repeatedly losing prescription drugs

It was your first visit to an especially uptight doctor, and you were unshaven and sloppily dressed to boot. What's more, the poison ivy on your forearm looked more than a little like track marks. You sensed his suspicion when you casually glanced at his syringes. After what seemed like an interminable series of questions, he reluctantly wrote you a thirty-count prescription for painkillers. And then, as soon as you got home, you accidentally dropped them in the toilet. How do you ask for more without looking like a drug-starved addict?

TACTICS

■ just a few, please

Call the office and try to sound respectable. Explain the situation but insist you don't need the full count of thirty: "I'm feeling a little better. I just need three to get me through the night." By requesting a small number, you look less like an addict. But, don't worry, you'll get plenty.

No one's writing a prescription for a ridiculous quantity like three pills.

■ bad reaction

Say the prescription gave you one of the bad side effects listed on the info packet. Act angry, making sure to include the phrase "I threw them out" in your tirade, as in, "That damned Vicodin made my teeth chatter so much I threw them out!" Demand an alternate drug.

DESPERATE MEASURES

Find a new doctor in a different town. This time around, dress conservatively and act frightened by the prospect of taking addictive painkillers. If you're clumsy enough to lose this second batch, call the office and say you threw them out because you heard they were highly addictive. Insist on an herbal or homeopathic remedy. Let the doctor calm you down. Reluctantly accept another prescription.

3. learning the person you're about to let go is in financial straits

You've been putting off firing the cleaning lady. It's not that she's untrustworthy or even incompetent. It's just that, well . . . she uses too much Pledge, she puts the TV remote in the phone charger, and she brings a lunch that makes the whole house smell like fish food. You bravely steel yourself for the task. Unfortunately, before you do the deed, you find her on the steps, sobbing. Her husband has been laid off and her sister's in the hospital. She hugs you with gratitude for the only job supporting her family right now. Then she picks up her rag and, sighing, resumes going at it with the Pledge.

■ **trump card**

Create a sob story of your own that makes her financial troubles look petty. Tell her your identity was stolen by a guy who opened up a line of credit to drive *your* company out of business. Unfortunately it's all legal so there's nothing you can do but spend the rest of your life paying off the loan. Tell her the bank controls your spending now, and you're only entitled to basic cable and store-brand ramen. If you can do so convincingly, request the receipt for the unopened Swiffer she bought because "every little bit helps."

bait and switch

You're not hurting anyone if you hook your housekeeper up with another employer to replace you. Sing her praises to your friends. If they're willing to give her a try, set up an appointment for the exact time she normally cleans your house. When she comes over, send her to your friend's house, saying, "That's the house you'll be cleaning from now on." If she seems confused or hurt, get out a map and point: "That house."

the non-firing firing

Rather than fire anyone, say you're simply unable to use the person's services at the present time for reasons that are out of your control. For example, you might call your trainer and tell him you've broken your leg. Or stop your housekeeper at the door, explaining that your apartment's a crime scene and the police won't let you touch anything. Or, for any hired hand, say that your company has transferred you to another state. It helps to be distraught; mention that the worst part of leaving is losing "great help like you."

4. deciding whether to tip

No one likes to feel like a cheapskate. No one likes to be a sucker, either. Somewhere in between lies the sweet spot of the perfect tip. But the questions don't end at when, who, and how much to tip. Sometimes you have only eighteen cents in your pocket. Other times, only a fifty. How do you make good tipping decisions under the watchful eye of a bellhop, valet parker, or maître d'?

TACTICS

▪ avoidance

It is possible to live your life avoiding a full 97 percent of all tippable services. Park your car in the street. Carry your own bags. Use the revolving door. Shun room service. Hail your own cab. Memorize your seat location before entering stadiums and concert halls. Last but not least, stand on your chair and wildly wave off mariachi bands and violinists who come within fifty feet of your dinner table.

▪ the smooth move

Roll or fold a single dollar bill into an extremely compact package. Jam this little puppy between two fingers or tuck it in the small of your palm. Practice "the smooth move": a quick, seamless transfer from your hand to the recipient's. For some reason, recipients will rarely complain about the value of the tip, perhaps because they associate the smooth move with the experienced, judicious tipper. Or perhaps it's because they don't have the time and patience to unwrap the tiny origami Cracker Jack prize you've handed them.

■ catch you on the rebound

Pepper conversations with hotel employees with winks, nods, and catchy phrases like "You take care of me, I take care of you," "Catch you on the rebound," and "I don't forget friends." This buys you time to sit in your hotel room with the free hotel pen and stationery and sweat out how in the hell you're going to divide twenty bucks among the eleven staffers you've made your buddies. If you're feeling unscrupulously cheap, wait until after the shift change to check out and don't make eye contact with any of the fresh faces holding open the doors to your get-away limo.

5. dealing with solicitors

While smooth-tongued telemarketers shilling Nigerian oil shares are easy to blow off, wide-eyed neighborhood kids selling Girl Scout cookies will always get you running for your wallet. Unfortunately most solicitors fall somewhere in between. You're not sure if they're neighborhood fund-raisers, legitimate salespeople, scammers, or, worst of all, thieves casing your house. How can you collect enough information to accurately make the call? The answer: You can't. You end up turning them down and feeling like a cold-hearted bastard, or paying up and feeling like a leech-ridden lake trout. But there is a way out: To quote the effeminate supercomputer from the classic comedy *War Games,* "The only winning move is not to play."

TACTICS

■ household crisis

The idea here is to demonstrate that your household is so out of control you can't possibly give the solicitor a minute of your time. As soon as you hear the doorbell ring, pick up a pot, put on a portable phone headset, and—if possible—grab a screaming baby or barking dog. Don a beleaguered expression and sprint to the door so you're out of breath as you open it. Then, carry on three conversations at once: "How can I help you—Harriet, no!—not you. Give Mommy a minute, dear. What did you say? We lost the account?!" Addressing the solicitor in an exasperated voice, say, "I'm sorry, can you come back at another time? Like maybe next year?"

■ i already talked to you

No matter what the solicitor says, insist that you already talked to him. Try to really believe it, so that his protests are returned with ever louder and angrier responses: "I know! You already told me that when you came by before!" At some point he will either believe you or decide you're crazy.

■ i don't live here

Saying "I don't live here" is an excellent opening move. If the solicitor is offering something to benefit the house or neighborhood, you have little reason to care. If not, your hand is still strengthened. To any request at all, you can now reply, "I don't have my wallet." If the solicitor says, "We can mail you the bill," respond, "I don't have an address. That's why I'm here."

6. getting naked too early at the doctor's office

Let's face it, the doctor's office is a virtual repository of awkwardness: patients guessing what others are there for; intimate questions about diet, sex, and bodily fluids; percussing, poking, and prodding while you squirm on a wax paper sheet. . . .

But none of these cringers is as bad as mistiming the moment of undress. The problem arises when there are no explicit instructions on disrobing. Perhaps the nurse has taken your blood pressure and, exiting, told you, "The doctor will be in shortly." Was that the signal? Will the doctor examine you promptly or ask questions first? Most doctors are impatient jerks. You don't want to ruffle yours by spending time undressing in front of him. But you certainly don't want him to walk in as your pants are halfway off and you're struggling to find the neckhole in that flimsy green paper gown. So you decide to get undressed. But if you're smart, you consider one of the following precautions.

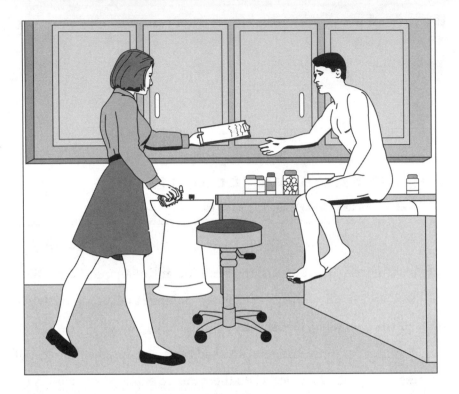

how much to undress

Conventional wisdom has it that underwear is the appropriate attire for the examination room. However, feel free to take the definition of underwear to its literal extreme. Underwear is under whatever you wear. Thus, if you're wearing a pair of shorts under your jeans, they're underwear. If you're wearing underwear on top of your jeans, the jeans are underwear. If it's a harsh winter and you're wearing the seven layers of Capilene turtlenecks recommended by Patagonia, you'll be six layers from embarrassment. Of course, the doc might have a hard time palpating that aggressive growth on your pancreas.

TACTICS

▪ early warning system

As you undress, lean against the door. Whoever attempts to enter will be temporarily rebuffed, giving you a moment to ask, "Who is it?" Should the intruder be a nurse, administrator, or attendant, shout, "One minute!" and put your clothes back on. Note: Do not place your head too close to the door, or you may find yourself naked and unconscious and susceptible to having a Polaroid of yourself exhibited in the staff lunchroom.

▪ wrap it up

Once fully undressed, sit on the examination table and unspool the wax paper, covering yourself like a take-home fish fillet. The wax paper will ward off goose bumps and shield you from the stares of nosy attendants and their ilk. Should a doctor enter, inform him that you were thoughtfully warming yourself so as not to shock his hands.

▪ weigh yourself

For some reason, scales and nudity go together. Boxers can stand naked on the scale on national television and no one seems to mind. If someone should enter, mutter, "Finally, an accurate weight," and, turning, add, "I haven't been on a Health-O-Meter since JV wrestling."

7. doing-it-yourself and regretting it

If you're a guy, there's no greater shame than paying someone to do something you could have done yourself. Actually, there is one greater shame: doing it yourself and screwing it up. But just because you're an incompetent boob doesn't mean you have to suffer through the smirks and lectures of a professional after you couldn't sharpen your lawn-mower blade, assemble a bicycle, or snap the egg-shaped head onto your kid's Fisher-Price doll.

So don't slink back to the store sheepishly. Pick one of the following approaches and march back with your head held high, confident that somebody smarter, better trained, and less "shaky handed" will fix things without subjecting you to a lengthy lecture or padding the bill with an "idiot fee."

TACTICS

▪ we try harder

Most stores will believe any complaint about a competitor. After all, it justifies their existence. Exploit their hubris by blaming your predicament on another store's advice, service, or merchandise. If you're currently in a boutique establishment, say, "I may have saved a few bucks at the discount place, but it sure wasn't worth it." If in a chain store, say, "I bought it at some tiny Mom and Pop joint. Those bozos probably only see one or two of these problems a year."

■ **the idiot friend**

Stroll into the store laughing and shaking your head. Lay the broken item on the counter, saying, "Look what a buddy of mine did. Poor slob's out of work so I thought I'd toss him an easy twenty bucks." If the employee still can't stop himself from launching into an annoying lecture, interrupt him with, "I know," "Preachin' to the choir, pal," or "Yeah. That's what I told my idiot friend."

■ **it came that way**

Take a tip from twentieth-century tyrants, who had a good run espousing the "one big lie" approach to fabrication. Upon entering a shop with a mangled bicycle, insist, "It came that way." In fact, don't merely say you didn't break it, say, "I never even touched it." Such an extreme position may make a believer out of a skeptical employee. And if it doesn't, no one's going to bother to lecture a crazy man.

■ **after hours**

Whenever possible, utilize the after-hours drop box. You won't be around for the rolled eyes and peals of insulting laughter. Plus, the phone makes it more difficult for know-it-all employees to point out all your stupid mistakes.

8. breaking up with your hairdresser

Despite talk about "revitalizing" hair and keeping it "alive and healthy," hair is actually dead keratin helices. But try telling that to your hairdresser. To him, hair is the very essence of life—not just a livelihood but a living expression of his ability to transform your deceased scalp extrusions into a powerful force for job promotion, socializing, and sexual pairing up.

Breaking up with your hairdresser is a major move. You are not only denigrating his talent, you are throwing out years of trust and intimacy. After all, your hairdresser is one of the few people privy to such sensitive information as your original hair color, your struggles with dandruff and "Spock ears," and your unscrupulous attempts at volumizing . . . not to mention your husband's last three affairs. How do you explain your new pixie cut the next time you run into him?

TACTICS

▪ tight budget

Hairstyling, along with powerboating and *People* subscriptions, is one of the three largest categories of discretionary spending. And even the snobbiest stylist will concede that food and shelter take precedence over layering and highlighting. Take advantage of this by pleading poverty. For credibility, connect your penury to a specific event, such as losing a lawsuit, getting fired, or blowing an appendix.

▪ garden of eden

Start by saying you no longer have time to trek all the way to the salon because your hectic lifestyle—carpooling, volunteering, a big promotion—has gotten the better of you. Then change gears and spend most of the conversation reminiscing about the days when you had the personal time to treat yourself the way you deserve: pedicures, yoga, and, of course, the best hairstylist in town. Wistfully ask if there's any chance his salon might move closer to you. Before he can respond, tell him, "You don't have to answer now. Just think about it. Please."

■ **family**

Family loyalties defy logic and explanation. No one can begrudge you for throwing a bone to your brother or sister or cousin, even if they are only minimally qualified. Say, "My kid brother became a hairstylist. He sucks. But, hey, he's my brother."

DESPERATE MEASURES

If the guilt of saying you've switched stylists is too much for you, try denying the betrayal. Of course, you'll need to explain why you don't look like *Homo habilis* though it's been half a year since you've been to the salon. One possibility is a mysterious medical condition: "My hair's growing really slowly. The doctors don't know why." Another is the industrial accident: "My hair was burned to the pate. Thank god, it seems to have found its way. Muscle memory, I think they call it?" Last, you can drop the word *chemotherapy*, which carries enough gravitas to chasten even the most suspicious stylist.

do not try this at home

Leaving one haircutter for another *in the same shop* is an advanced move that requires foresight, teamwork, and balls of shot-peened titanium. Nothing in this book should be construed as to recommend or even condone such a maneuver.

LIFE IS SO MUCH EASIER when you're in control, when you're the boss. Perhaps because of this, the previous situations were imbued with a certain element of calm. No such luck in the following section, where your self-esteem, social standing, and financial security are always on the precipice.

3 the workplace:

SALVAGING YOUR DIGNITY FROM NINE TO FIVE

FEW THINGS ARE MORE AWKWARD than work. You spend hours a day side by side with people who aren't even your friends. More likely than not, they're your enemies. And they're watching to make sure you don't get too far ahead or fall too far behind.

But what exactly are they watching? What is it that you *do*? According to the most recent figures, 38 percent of all employed Americans had the title "associate." Associated with what? A company, presumably, but one so hazy on its employees' roles, it can't even think of a better title than "associate."

Vague relationships, murky roles . . . with work boundaries as fuzzy as they are, it's inevitable you'll cross somebody or something somewhere, somehow. So here are some fuzzbusters to keep you happily ensconced in that big corner office of your mind.

1. carrying on a workplace romance

Not all workplace affairs need to be discreet. If you're a human resources manager and happen to hit it off with a hunky salesman from
a separate division, you can carry on a red-hot romance with nary an
awkward moment other than the annual company "fun run." Unfortunately your odds of meeting someone in a distant division are about
the same as your chances of marrying Mr. May from the naked fire-
man calendar in your cubicle.

Instead your affair is likely to be with an assistant, a boss, or
someone looking for the same promotion as you. It will likely meet the
standards of thousands of successful harassment suits and force you to
lie to everyone you encounter. But, hey, you're in love. Or at least getting laid. So let's see what we can do to help.

TACTICS

■ joint projects

Your best move is to get yourselves assigned to the same task. If successful, you can hang out in conference rooms hour after hour, discussing such project details as where you'll go to dinner, what birth control you'll use, and why you didn't call. Volunteer for a project best suited for exactly two staffers. Consider printing up enormous flow charts and marketing posters to paper over interior windows that might otherwise reveal your sweaty wrestling on the conference table.

■ travel

If a joint project is impossible, attempt to coordinate travel plans. If you both have upcoming meetings in the Midwest, for example, you might win points with the travel office by "reluctantly" sharing cars and lodging. Keep in mind that implausible destinations such as Caribbean resorts are only potential business trips if your company makes scuba gear, paper drink umbrellas, or retroviral medications.

■ get "buried"

Coming in early and staying late can afford you the privacy needed to carry on a workplace affair. Plant the seeds of your new schedule by repeatedly rubbing your temples and telling coworkers how "buried" you are. If you're feeling especially frisky, you can even pull an all-nighter. Just remember to produce something besides sore groin muscles and strange cubicle odors to show for your commitment to the company.

■ hate

Explain away your hours together by complaining about your paramour, disguising your love as hate. When he calls, point to your phone and say, "Look at that. Shit-for-brains is asking me for more help with his stupid project." If you run into others on your way to his office, say, "Shit-for-brains fucked things up again. I'm going to be all over him until he gets it right."

2. ending a workplace romance

Even trickier than carrying on an office courtship is ending one without permanently damaging your ego or career. Disabuse yourself of any notions of mutual civility or professionalism. This will be a fight to the death. So stop working on that "killer app" and start channeling the killer ape inside you.

TACTICS

■ well-laid trap

If you used some of the above strategies for carrying on your affair, there's an added bonus: You may now use them to *end* the affair.

Although your liaison is now public knowledge, claim you were swayed by his looks alone. Refer back to the hate ruse: "I always said he was an incompetent idiot, and I stand by it." Pull out the phony flow charts and crude marketing posters of the previous section's "joint projects" tactic as proof of his incompetence.

■ start spreading the news

If your paramour has seniority at work, exposure of the affair presents a bigger problem for him than for you. As soon as you sense the romance souring, tell as many people as you can about the affair. This not only gives you ammo for a harassment suit if you're fired, but it also means that any derogatory comments or bad assignments will be seen as sour grapes or revenge on his part. Played right, this move will free you with a promotion and a raise to boot.

■ move up the food chain

If, on the other hand, it is you who is the senior employee, you're going to find yourself hog-tied in the revenge and sour grapes departments. Before you're slaughtered, begin an affair with somebody senior to you. Publicize the new affair and earn immunity all over again. Avoid the "office slut" label by dressing conservatively and wearing your hair in a bun.

3. falling asleep in a meeting

Work is numbing when you're well rested. When you're tired and forced to sit through three-hour meetings about the corporate mission statement, it can be agony. Luckily for you, the body has developed a defense mechanism against such anguish: a subconscious state scientists term "sleep." Unluckily for you, sleep itself can be awkward, causing involuntary kicking and swatting, "sleep face," and drool that pools on the table and smears the pie charts in your presentation.

TACTICS

■ frontload

Be especially active at the start of a meeting. Ask questions, challenge assumptions, and lead discussion back to "core values." Be sure to gesture wildly, jumping out of your seat with enthusiasm or disgust, so that you will have imprinted your vitality into everyone's memory long after your voice has been silenced by beta waves and thoughts of swimsuit models.

■ hide-and-sleep

If your office permits casual attire, take advantage of certain clothes that hide the physical manifestations of snoozing. A hat with a large brim can cast a handy shadow. Sunglasses will do it one better. An acrylic shirt will cause drool to bead up and harmlessly roll off your body. A kilt, while unconventional, can provide men with valuable "growing room" for one of the stranger effects of REM sleep.

■ front and center

A counterintuitive but effective precaution: When selecting a seat in an auditorium-style meeting, grab one in the front row. This tactic is similar to frontloading, since a bold move early on signals to everyone that you are engaged, interested, and serious. However, since all anyone can see of you is the back of your head, you are free to tune out and catch a few winks. Nodding off may even fool others into thinking you vehemently agree with the speaker. If there's a video projector, try to position yourself as close as possible to its beam of light. Not even the presenter will be able to see through the 4500 lumen glow to distinguish whether you are nodding along or just nodding off.

■ the thinker

At all meetings, make a habit of adopting the pose made famous by sculptor/napper August Rodin. That way, when you do fall asleep, you will appear to be lost in deep thought, coaxing great new ideas from behind your forehead.

■ wake-up phrase

A handy addition to the Thinker. Cultivate a waking phrase, something easy to remember even when your brain is stuck in first gear. The concept is simple. When a loud noise or protracted silence awakens you with the horrible realization that you're about to be discovered, force your eyes open and shout the preselected phrase. Try something along the lines of, "I've got it! We need to get back to core values! Let's pull out the mission statement." Then stride to the bathroom to try to figure out what the hell's going on and freshen up your sleep face.

4. greeting the same person repeatedly

You probably walk down the office hall some twenty times a day—for meetings, coffee, lunch, the bathroom, office supplies, or just to stretch your legs. During these excursions, there's always one particular coworker who seems to be on the identical hallway schedule. The first encounter of the morning is pleasant enough: greetings, sports banter, and other harmless small talk. The second encounter is a bit more strained. You might echo something mentioned earlier, offer up another observation about that exciting football game, or simply smile disarmingly and raise your eyebrows the way our simian ancestors did when swinging past each other in the jungle. But by the third encounter, you're deep in the awkward zone, willing to do anything to avoid the Hallway Stalker.

TACTICS

■ look busy

This is the default tactic, practiced instinctively by all of us. But most people don't fully commit to the stratagem. For real credibility, you need three things: speed, props, and shouting.

Speed implies preoccupation and urgency, with the added benefit of minimizing time of exposure. Fast walking won't cut it. You need to run. If running down the hall feels strange, that's the whole point. Only someone facing a critical deadline would sprint in wingtips.

Props tell a story: Why is this person running? It must have to do with the stacks of folders, the overhead projector, or the bag of Cheez Doodles he is holding.

Shouting lets the stalker know your urgency involves other people in the office. Direct your shouts to unseen coworkers: "I found them! I found the missing files! Keep him on the phone, Sharon!"

■ breaking news

Direct your small talk toward things in constant flux, such as stock indices, traffic conditions, or international sports scores. At subsequent encounters, you can break the tension with updates: "The Wilshire 5000 dropped a point!" or "Wen Xu just got cut from the Chinese gymnastics team!"

MISMATCHED SMALL TALK

Passing quickly in the hall, you might occasionally find yourself responding, "Pretty good" to "What's up?" or "Not much" to "How's it going?" Such inappropriate replies are telltale signs of contempt for your coworkers. Instead, try answering questions with questions. For example, "How you doin'?" is a reasonable reply to almost any insincere greeting.

■ detours

Is there another way to get where you're going? Take the road less traveled: freight elevator, fire exit, or mail chute. . . . But be sure you're the only one with this idea. If fate should place you together on the loading dock, you might find yourself the recipient of a restraining order.

5. getting fired

If you suspect you're going to be fired soon, there are steps you can take to minimize the attendant pain and embarrassment, from stealthily minimalizing your office decor to stocking up on paper and toner cartridges for your résumé.

However, most of the time companies surprise you with such a move. In these cases, there is little you can do to avoid the awkwardness of the security guard–escorted march of shame from your cubicle to the exit. The best you can do is minimize the *subsequent* damage: the prying questions, pitying remarks, and unhelpful offers of assistance from spouses, friends, and family.

TACTICS

▓ a wrinkle in time

It will take a while for news of your failure to trickle down to friends and family. During this "wrinkle in time," begin constructing your own path to the present. Approach friends and tell them you're thinking of quitting. Ask them to read your resignation letter. Debate the merits of resigning versus "forcing them to fire me, so I get a cushy severance package." Tell them to keep the news secret; you "don't want to blindside the company." By the time the "wrinkle" straightens out, your friends will have no choice but to believe your rosy version of the events surrounding your departure.

▓ the transfer

Friends and family generally have no appreciation for the size and complexity of the company you work for. If you think you can land a new job within a few weeks, tell people you've been transferred to a different branch of the company. You're no longer working downtown at the telecommunications division. You're now working at the energy division—specifically, the gas station down the street.

6. waging an unspoken war

The office environment is a fertile petri dish for petty disputes between employees. When you have no control over major decisions—such as how much you are paid—small decisions such as whether to keep the window open, what radio station to listen to, or how high to set the thermostat take on the utmost importance. Unfortunately the silent wars that develop over these matters tend to spiral out of control, leading to awkward confrontations. What do you say to a coworker when she catches you, clad in a parka and wool hat, turning the thermostat down to forty-eight degrees?

TACTICS

■ what war?

Your first instinct might be to cite history. After all, your coworker has been setting the thermostat to ninety degrees in repeated attempts to bake you out of the office.

Don't do it. Citing history is an admission of vengeful intent. Instead, cultivate an ingenuous smile and inform your coworker you were a tad warm. Would it be all right if you lowered the temperature a bit? Either she will join your charade and the two of you will be forced to compromise . . . or she will foolishly cite history and reveal her own vengeful motives, making herself look as petty and pathetic as you secretly are.

▪ take the other side

When caught with your hands in the cookie jar, one easy out is to say you were putting them back. By pretending to be on the other side of a conflict, you defuse accusations before they arise. In the thermostat example, you might say, "Somebody keeps setting this to fifty degrees. It's been so bad I've had to bring this parka and cap to work. I hope we find out who's doing it."

▪ company policy

Avoid being pegged as a "Me, Myself, and I" person. Drape your self-serving actions with the flag of the firm. "In the company handbook, it says employees should look for opportunities to save money. Our heating bills are unnecessarily burdened by every degree over sixty-eight. While I personally find this low temperature unpleasant, I feel happy knowing there's more money for our management, stockholders, and cash reserves."

7. sitting next to your boss on an airplane

Spending time with the boss outside the office is like seeing a parent naked. There's just something fundamentally wrong about it. So, when you find yourself sitting together on a twelve-hour flight to Taipei, it's time to pull out all the stops and take protective measures . . . or pray for a water landing in the north Pacific.

TACTICS

■ the penny pincher

Evasive moves can be made under the guise of saving the company money. If you're seated in business class, ask about a downgrade to economy. If you're in economy class, ask if they've overbooked and volunteer your seat for a freebie on a later flight. You may even be able to book on a discount airline or get a lower price by choosing a route with plane changes in Anchorage, Seoul, and Osaka.

■ the good parent

Preoccupy your boss with books, puzzles, and computer games. Make sure to load up a big carry-on with the latest and greatest toys, ideally items the boss has seen advertised on TV. When his attention flags, pull out something new. Watch his eyes light up as you show him how to program a playlist on your iPod or burn a CD on your computer. If necessary, ask an attendant for extra cookies to stave off "the crabbies." As you approach your destination, tell your boss, "We're almost there," and remind him what a great boss he's been.

DESPERATE MEASURES

Even the most hardened taskmaster recognizes the precedence certain bodily functions take over chitchat or even preparation for a meeting. Shortly after takeoff, inform your boss that you're not feeling well and head to the toilet, grabbing a few magazines en route. Then stay there the whole flight. Since you're the first occupant, it should be clean and odor free. As a bonus, you'll have considerably more legroom than you would in your regular seat.

8. sharing a hotel room
with a coworker

Travel is rough. You have to rush to the airport, wait in lines, sit in a cramped seat with bad food (or no food at all), suffer jet lag, spend countless days away from home, and drag around presentations, samples, and brochures. Aside from collecting frequent flyer miles, the only good thing about travel is vegging out in a hotel room.

Unfortunately, with corporate cost-cutting, you might be forced to share that sacred space with a coworker—often someone you've little in common with besides similar size cubicles in the office.

TACTICS

■ **dracula**

Render your incompatibility moot by altering your sleep schedule to minimize hours spent together. If your meetings are early in the day or late in the afternoon, become nocturnal, sleeping only when the sun's up. At night, after your roommate turns in, the room is effectively yours. Walk around in your underwear, watch porn, and read all four sections of *USA Today* on the toilet with impunity.

■ homesteading

Like an 1860s pioneer, prove up your claim to the room by spreading around possessions and making "improvements."

After entering the room, quickly place personal items such as underwear, family photos, and used tissues over bureaus, nightstands, and armchairs, scattering your other belongings throughout the drawers and closets. Unwrap and use every soap, sewing kit, shampoo/conditioner, and bottle of mouthwash, availing yourself generously of each. Don the shower cap, fill the ice bucket with ice and water and soak your feet. Finally, buff your shoes with the complimentary cloth while doodling on all the stationery.

No doubt all this work has made you tired. Grab the extra blankets and pillows from the closet, build a giant nest on the bed of your choice, and lay down on your back, tightly gripping the remote and flicking furiously through all the channels. When you finally nod off, make sure that your head is propped up to maximize snoring and drooling, and that the channel selector is parked on the hotel info station.

If you follow these or similar steps, your unfortunate roommate will feel like a freegrazer and will move on to more welcoming pastures in the lobby.

■ bad roommate

Be generally offensive. Clip your toenails onto the carpet. Shout into the phone. Fart with abandon. Then leave it to your coworkers to do the tricky, behind-the-scenes negotiating with the office travel manager to find you a room of your own.

WORK CERTAINLY HAS ITS SHARE of awkward moments, but at least the others involved have an incentive to keep things professional. Our next topic lacks this advantage and adds a complicating factor: the frustration of being oh-so-close to ecstasy.

4 sex:

GETTING TO YES, YES, YESSSS!

LIKE PEANUT BUTTER AND CHOCOLATE, awkwardness and sex have an intrinsic compatibility. Strict translations of Genesis refer to "the tree of embarrassment" and most paleolithic cave drawings are now considered to have been elaborate excuses for poor sexual performance. Science points to a reason: gamma-aminobutyrate, the brain chemical responsible for embarrassment, makes up a full 85 percent of the composition of semen.

Some experts would have you see awkwardness as part of the process rather than a problem to be addressed. These experts are wrong. They are homely academics who never get laid and secretly wish that human social habits were closer to those of the wildly promiscuous Bonobo pygmy chimp.

So while you may never experience the exquisite satisfaction of the average Bonobo, by following the advice below you will minimize impediments to your own sense of fulfillment.

1. yelling out the wrong name during sex

There's nothing wrong with fantasizing about others during sex. Maybe you can't stop thinking about that buxomy waitress at dinner. Maybe the guy huffing and puffing on top of you looks a lot like Quasimodo.

The problem arises when your redlining limbic system has trouble coordinating the fantasy in your head with the vocalizations from your mouth.

Luckily, if you learn the steps below, your more highly evolved cerebrum can bail out that horny limbic system and let it get back to doing what it does best: bumping and grinding to exhaustion.

TACTICS

■ morph it

Chances are your partner will be a bit unclear on what you said, espe-cially if you've uttered the wrong name only once. If you can catch yourself after the first slip up, morph it into an acceptable homonym.

For example, if you accidentally yell, "Claude!" turn it into, "Oh, god!" This also works for Todd, Maude, Rod, and Fawn. "Sarah!" can become "Allah!"; "Noah!" can become "Jehovah!"; and "Jesus!" can stay the same. "Mary!" can become "Marry me!" Although that might, of course, present a greater problem.

■ "get the hell out of here!"

If a name eludes morphing, add, "Get the hell out of here!" as in "Jonathan . . . get the hell out of here!" Immediately turn to your mys-tified partner and explain: "I saw someone in the window. It looked like Jonathan. He's my old boyfriend. I'm sorry if I startled you, but that creep's been stalking me."

■ pet names

After yelling the wrong name, coyly inform your lover it's your personal name for his penis (or her vagina). An additional benefit: You are now free to shout the name as much as you like during future sexual activities. A caveat: You will look particularly unimaginative if your fantasy partner's name is Dick or Pussy.

The catalog of human mating cues is vast and complex, with many subtle and hard-to-read elements. There are frequent and awkward communication glitches, from refused flowers to unreturned phone calls to incest.

   One of the most common errors is mistakenly believing someone is coming on to you. You kick up your heels and begin the mating dance, only to find yourself alone on the parquet. This is especially awkward when the other person is happily and vocally attached, engaged, or married. It's awkward in the extreme when she's attached, engaged, or married to your buddy.

TACTICS

■ turn it around

As soon as the person says, "I'm engaged," say, "I know. Wait a second—you didn't think I was asking you out, did you?" Become indignant. Match or exceed her anger, as if it was she who plunged you into the current state of awkwardness. Even if moments earlier you caressed her back and whispered, "This couch folds out," you should now take offense that she mistook it for a come-on. "I was just talking about the friggin' couch, you sex-obsessed nympho!"

■ second person plural

Take advantage of the fact that, in English-speaking areas outside the Deep South, there is no easy way to distinguish between the second person singular (you) and the second person plural (you). Insist that your "you" referred to both her and her husband. For example, if you said, "Would you like to ride the Tunnel of Love with me?" you can now explain that you love the ride for its own sake, but it's much more exciting if there's a couple kissing nearby.

■ **make it about the partner**

If you've asked for her phone number, explain that you need it to get in touch with her husband. If she responds that you don't know her husband, explain that that's the problem. You have no way to get in touch with him.

DESPERATE MEASURES

If you're less worried about offending the person you're coming on to than the people she might tell, you might say, "Are you kidding? I'd never date a dog like you." Or you might trade one embarrassment for another, telling her, "I have absolutely no interest in you or, for that matter, any woman. At least not one that's alive."

3. breaking up with someone suddenly beset by misfortune

You're just about to dump your too-short, lazy, sweaty-footed boyfriend when you find out his dad died. You can't call things off now. You'd look heartless. In fact, he and his dad were so close that it might be months before you can make a clean break. By which time the green-eyed Irish poet you met last week will have returned to Kilkenny.

TACTICS

■ **go invertebrate**

Use your boyfriend's bad news to convince him you're a weak, blub-bery, hyperemotional wreck. When he tells you about his dad, pretend your world has fallen apart. Cry to the point that he spends more time consoling you than dealing with his own grief. Don't stop sobbing until he leaves you.

■ **"our tragedies"**

Bring up bad news of your own, but bad news well short of his tragedy. When he tells you his dad died, tell him that your cat died. Use the phrase "our tragedies" at every opportunity. He will steadily become incensed that you're putting your cat on par with his father. After he dumps you, tell friends, "I was very supportive when his dad died, but he couldn't be bothered to give me an ounce of sympathy for a cat I'd owned since college. I can't be with an insensitive jerk like that."

4. undressing prematurely

If sex is making stew, women are crock pots and men are microwaves. This imbalance sometimes leads to serious errors of timing. One of the least discussed—but most traumatic—is premature undressing.

After dinner, your female companion might make some vaguely sexual reference and head to the bathroom, presumably to disrobe and install a complicated birth control apparatus. Not one to miss your moment, you furiously undress and recline on the couch, only to watch her emerge fully clothed but wearing eyeglasses instead of itchy contact lenses—and all the better to watch your blushing body try to will itself invisible.

TACTICS

■ go nudist

Remove all sexual connotations from your nakedness. Nonchalantly ask if she wants to watch TV or sit out on the fire escape. If she's appalled by your lack of clothes, proselytize, referring to the famous Nudist Manifesto of 1968. Eventually, give in to her concerns, saying, "Being with you is more important than being in harmony with the immutable laws of Nature and God."

■ healthy habits

If you were outdoors that day, ask her to examine you for ticks. If you had significant exposure to the sun, say you're worried about skin cancer. If you've been indoors, face the wall, lean forward, and ask her to check your spine for the telltale "asymmetric smile" of scoliosis. Use your health concerns as a form of foreplay, telling her, "I want to be around you a long, long time."

■ toxicology

Run to the shower, frantically explaining that your skin began burning moments ago and you suspect the shifty-eyed guy at the back of the movie theater was a chemically armed terrorist. If she insists she doesn't feel anything, breathe a sigh of relief and chalk up your itchies to the off-brand pack of mountain meadow dryer sheets you foolishly bought because you had a coupon.

5. regretting that you've asked about a partner's fantasy

Near the top of the ladder of intimacy is a desire to learn the most intimate sexual fantasies of your partner. The trouble comes when your inquiry draws out a scenario that exceeds your most disturbing expectations . . . perhaps something with a shoe or an animal or what you thought was a highly specialized orifice.

If your boyfriend, fiancé, or spouse excitedly divulges a horrific desire, you need to be very careful in your response. Simply going along can quash your own sense of decency and self worth. Telling him you find the fantasy revolting might offend him or make your enthusiasm from just moments before seem insincere—not to mention leave him feeling perpetually unfulfilled, his growing desire leading to infidelity, insanity, or incarceration.

TACTICS

■ **incompetence**

Pretend you're really excited about his fantasy, but perform it as incompetently as possible. Unless the fantasy specifically calls for it, robotic, painful, and sloppy execution is key. Suggest that the fantasy is physiologically impossible. Say, "When I'm down here, I can't reach up there. I'd need to have arms, like, eight feet long." Eventually, your partner will reshape his worldview and successfully mourn the fantasy. Note: This tactic is more likely to work if you are expert in the other aspects of your sex life so your partner suspects that no one—not even Linda "Deep Throat" Lovelace or a horny octopus—could implement his plan.

■ death by association

Concoct fictitious accounts of unappealing persons who have shared your partner's obsession. Say, "No kidding? You're into the carrot thing?" and describe a grotesque, elderly, overweight circus freak known for his love of that very act.

■ in the family

Studies have proven that most sexual preferences have a strong genetic component. One set of twins separated at birth shared nothing in common except that they both enjoyed wearing tube socks and watching stand-up comedy while copulating. Remind your partner that his parents and siblings most likely share his fantasy and may even be practicing it this very moment. If this only piques his interest, you've got a bigger problem than you thought.

ONE SAVING GRACE to sexual awkwardness is that, in the worst of circumstances, you'll never see the other person again. If only that were true with our next topic, where embarrassments can last a lifetime.

5 friends and family:

KEEPING YOUR WORST FROM THOSE WHO KNOW YOU BEST

YOU CAN'T CHOOSE YOUR FAMILY. You have a bit of choice when it comes to friends, but it's more a history of choices than anything relating to who you are today or what you want for your future. So it's no surprise that you're surrounded by annoying losers who cramp your style and ruin your fun.

Nonetheless, you're lucky if you have any friends and family at all. Based on all the times you've blown them off, failed to support them, manipulated, lied to, and hurt them, you're lucky they didn't abandon you years ago. And that's exactly what makes it so tough now. You've already used your best lines on them. They know all your tricks, and they're sick of giving you third and fourth chances.

So study this chapter like JFK Jr. on his final attempt at the bar. Because, lame as these people are, they're the only friends and family you've got.

1. skipping out on an event

Maybe it's a hassle. Maybe you'd forgotten about it until just now. Maybe you'd rather be playing golf. Whatever the reason, you've decided not to attend Aunt Jennie's eightieth birthday party. Screw her stupid son and his uptight wife and those snotty cousins whose names you can't remember. Now, if you could just keep them from plucking your guilt strings . . .

TACTICS

■ plausible ignorance

Recall how you were invited. Was it by phone? Mail? E-mail? Because, short of an in-person or over-the-phone confirmation, you can plausibly claim ignorance. Sometimes mail gets lost. Have you recently moved? Were you out of town and using a neighbor to hold your correspondence? Perhaps someone's been stealing your mail. (After you fail to show, you might ask your hosts if they noticed a strange person at the event.) Have you had problems with your answering machine? Does your voice mail system have some bugs? Does your spam filter go hog wild? Every one of these is a credible excuse, particularly for "save the date" events.

A key to employing this tactic is the angry follow-up phone call. Make sure to beat your disappointed hosts to the phone. Act peeved and hurt. Sarcastically say, "Thanks for the invitation. Did you forget to mail it, or do you just hate the sight of me?" When they insist that they did send it, turn your anger on your predetermined scapegoat: "Damned junk e-mail filter! When is Bill Gates gonna finally get that software right?"

■ look ahead

This wonderful method convinces others that you had a tremendous desire to attend but were confounded by extraordinary circumstances totally beyond your control. And it does so without even requiring you to think of an excuse!

Whenever someone mentions your absence from an event, move on to your excitement about the *next* get-together. When your Dad complains, "We didn't see you July fourth," tell him, "I'm just glad I'm going to see you at Thanksgiving. Now *that's* something to be thankful for."

■ call their bluff

Tell others you can't attend because you have no money or nowhere to stay. The ball's in their court: Unless they're willing to shell out for your transportation or put you up themselves, you won't be able to make it.

The risks are obvious but the potential payoff is huge. If others fail to come through, you'll have a guilt-free weekend. They, on the other hand, might be too guilt-ridden to invite you to the next gathering.

■ rock solid

With once-in-a-lifetime events like christenings and funerals, you need something rock-solid: the grave illness or death of an immediate family member or, possibly, yourself. After missing your aunt's funeral, tell your relative, "I was deathly ill. It's lucky you didn't have two funerals to go to."

2. being asked to appraise someone's boyfriend/girlfriend

If a guy asks you for your opinion of his girlfriend, it's a bad sign. Nine times out of ten he's looking for a reason to dump her. But that one time can really bite you. Even if you've been pals for twenty years, if he sticks with this loser chick you'll never water-ski at his summer house again.

There's always "damning with faint praise," but for most of the dumb or weak-willed types who want your opinion, such subtlety won't cut it. You'll need something stronger.

TACTICS

■ ask leading questions

Strike a disinterested, professorial tone and tell your friend you need more information before you can render an opinion. Then begin a barrage of leading questions that paint a picture of the girlfriend as a miserable pain in the ass. Try, "Have you ever known her to be a skinflint?" and "Has she won any beauty contests?" and "Does she ever, ever get you upset?" After each reply, shake your head and murmur gravely. Do not make verbal judgments. Your silence will speak volumes.

■ i could be wrong

Cover your ass by praising the girlfriend but note that your opinion is not widely shared. Say, "I think she's wonderful, but frankly I'm mystified that nobody else does. Why does everyone else hate her? I don't get it." Bolster the majority opinion by conceding that you're usually wrong on these matters.

■ the judge of character

Strongly recommend that your friend talk to somebody else, someone who is a better judge of character. "Brainstorm" to come up with just the right person to ask, and then pretend to come up with someone you've secretly been thinking about all along . . . someone who hates her like the devil. "Hey, what about Jim? Jim's a great judge of character. You've got to talk to Jim."

■ **the positive negative**

Praise the girlfriend for all her unflattering qualities: "She tells it like it is. When she told off your mother the other day, I was so impressed." Or, "She's classy. She spends money like an heiress." Or, "She's so independent. She's totally cool with having no friends."

3. getting caught regifting

It's 5:30 and you're already late to your friend Samantha's birthday party. No time to hit the stores. And who needs to when you've got closets full of potential presents from thoughtless or tasteless gift-givers past? There's the vomit green blender, the stinky Brookstone cashew pillow, the "found objects" frame, the cruddy bottle of Merlot, and that dusty copy of *Oh, the Places You'll Go!* that hasn't gone anywhere. Until now. Happy birthday, Samantha!

Unfortunately, at the party another guest notices the inscription in the book. It's made out to you, and it's dated last year.

TACTICS

■ **i liked it so much . . .**

Tell everyone it's your favorite book (or pillow or Merlot or whatever). It means so much to you that you've made it your standard gift. You've bought so many copies over the years that you must have accidentally switched one with your own. To back up your story, dash to the bookstore immediately after the party and purchase another copy. Wrap it in week-old newspaper before delivering it so they think it was purchased days earlier.

■ **save a tree**

Act as though your regifting is part of a master ecological plan. Tell your friend she can enjoy the book for a while, but add, "Please, just as I did, pass it on to someone else when you're done." Tailor your party etiquette to match your "green" attitude. Collect discarded wrapping paper, carve your initials into the bottom of your plastic cup for reuse, and talk about the miracle of the composting toilet.

■ **the good ol' days**

They don't make 'em like they used to. At least not the gift you just gave. Sure, you could've run out and bought a brand-new one. But those are made in China now. They're mass produced, disposable crap. Yours was made in Japan, where they practically invented Total Quality Control. It's built of reinforced, overbuilt metal. And even though it's got some wear and tear, it'll last ten times as long as a new one.

the gift you don't deserve

If you receive a present for an occasion that never comes to pass (like an engagement gift for a broken-off wedding), you may regift with abandon. If caught, say you did not deserve the gift and the only way to purge your guilt was to give it to someone who does.

4. not calling when you're in town

You and your husband have been planning a romantic trip out west for some time. On the agenda: the finest museums, the best restaurants, and a great hotel room. Not on the agenda: Aunt Frieda and Uncle Nat, who have kind hearts but a musty guest room and endless, dull stories of swap-meet plunder. Unfortunately, walking out of your five-star hotel, you lock eyes with the septuagenarian swap-aholics on their way to a downtown flea market. They are confused and hurt. Why didn't their favorite niece call to say she'd be in town?

TACTICS

■ unscheduled stop

Sadly inform your relatives that you are not, strictly speaking, visiting. The windows blew out on your plane and they had to put you up here while they dealt with the problem. But the airline has finally boarded up the windows and you're back on your way to your original destination: a small resort between Shangri-La and Atlantis.

■ "i knew it!"

Scream with glee, embrace your relatives, and turn to your husband, saying, "I knew if we hung around downtown long enough we'd see them!" Explain that you've been planning this for weeks. "We just wanted to see the looks on your faces when you ran into us. Priceless."

■ "where the hell am i?"

Act disoriented. Say, "Where the hell am I?" and "What are you two doing here?" When they insist that they live there, rebut their contention, using an archaic or alternate name for the locale. For example, when in San Francisco, you might say, "But this is the Bay Area. You live in San Francisco. When they explain, stick to your guns. Shake your head and furrow your brow. Eventually, allow yourself to be convinced that they are right. But angrily blame the city for "not standardizing its damned nomenclature."

■ extended stay

Explain that you haven't called because you'll be in town for a long stretch and you've set aside lots of time to visit with them. If they insist on your staying with them, tell them you don't want to be a burden, since you expect to be around for a very long time—months, possibly longer. At the very end of your trip, call them, feigning distress. Explain that an emergency has come up at home, something vague but scary: a septic backup, an electrical fire, or the levee needing more sandbags.

DESPERATE MEASURES

Refuse to acknowledge that you are yourself. Talk in a foreign language, contort your face, and walk with a hunch. If your relatives confront you, shout at them in badly broken English: "I not him! I dream of a man who look like me but he *from* America. That is the man I want to be!" Shake their hands vigorously and move on, muttering, "Yes, yes, I love America."

5. failing to return a call

In the early days of telephony, missing a call carried little psychic baggage. Not so today. The guilt begins when the caller ID displays the dreaded digits, revs up while you screen the long-winded message and pathetic pleas for a quick response, and festers during your days and weeks of indecision. You wonder, "Should I call back? I don't want to, but if I wait it could be worse." So you wait.

Things gets uglier when the other person calls again. And again. And uglier still when you suddenly need a favor from him. Now you're in big trouble. You're going to need a cool head, creativity, and the balls of a Reform Party cold caller.

TACTICS

■ phone tag

Phone Tag is a handy phrase that should become a standard part of your return call lexicon. No matter how remiss you've been, Phone Tag implies that both parties have put in effort and are feeling frustration. Use it liberally to bathe short-term hurt with the rosy glow of an innocent childhood game. (It matters little that this version of Tag more closely resembles the version of Hide and Seek where everyone ditched the seeker and went off to play in Melvin's pool.)

■ e-xcuse

Send an e-mail beginning with the line, "We can't seem to connect by phone." A mere 1K of text magically shifts blame from you to an ill-defined entity, leaving the recipient wondering whether his phone, your phone, his service, your service, or the entire worldwide telecommunications infrastructure is at fault.

■ encyclopedia brown

Call and say, "I'm trying to solve a mystery. I've been looking at some chicken scratch on a piece of cardboard that's been lying around for months. I'm not sure if I wrote it or somebody else did, but it seems remotely possible that it's your name. Any chance you called me two or three months ago? . . . "

■ **"I'm back"**

Almost as powerful as Phone Tag, "I'm back" says you were unavailable to receive or return calls for an indeterminate period of time. Simply say, "I'm back. I saw that you called," and move on with the discussion. If asked where you're back from, sigh loudly and say, "All over the place. But I'm back now. Hopefully back for good."

6. getting rid of guests

All cultures place great importance on the tradition of hosting. The Hawaiians offer their guests generous helpings of pit-cooked pig and colorful necklaces strung with native flowers. The Japanese lavish guests with disturbingly big-eyed dolls and tiny sushi refrigerator magnets. The people of Yemen present visitors with crates of khat leaves, which, while mildly mood enhancing, carry a ten-year term for trafficking in countries signatory to the 1971 International Agreement on Psychotropic Substances.

And what custom, in return, is a guest obligated to perform? Well, primarily . . . to leave. Perhaps not immediately, but soon. And certainly well before he has gone through two sets of alkaline batteries on the TV remote control.

Unfortunately, many modern-day guests have lost touch with the ancient tradition of leaving. Which means you may find yourself forced to employ one of the following customs.

TACTICS

▪ disruptive hobbies

Do you practice the drums? Do you play the accordion? Have you tried the bagpipes? What about skeet shooting? These are all pastimes you'd do well to take up. Also consider sunrise photography, chainsawing, hammering, in-home auctioneering, and hydrogen sulfide (egg rot) research.

▪ radical politics

Otherwise-reasonable people have latent political "hot buttons" that can be exploited to hasten their departure. Divine the political preferences of your guest by slowly flipping through the AM radio channels and watching his face. When it registers revulsion, stop, turn up the volume, and say, "Damn right!" to the radio, pumping your fist in the air enthusiastically.

Bolster this political "poison pill" by actively supporting positions your guest loathes. Purchase and subscribe to radical publications. Decorate your house with NAMBLA or "White Power" posters. Ask for help stuffing fundraising envelopes for "the movement." For extra help with the food budget, consider invoking the names of hated politicians in your prayers before meals.

■ crowd 'em out

Invite additional guests to your domicile, preferably ones you trust to leave promptly when asked.

The prospect of competing with other moochers for limited household resources will frustrate your problem guests, perhaps driving them on to greener pastures. Sometimes, however, a beautiful thing happens. By "holding a mirror" to their faces, you will awaken long repressed memories of courtesy and manners, causing guests to apologize and leave behind parting gifts like bottles of wine or money for gas, water, and electric bills.

■ lockout

Set the stage by hinting to your guests that you may be forced to leave town for several days. (They will doubtless plan to stay since no similar hints have pried them from your residence thus far.)

In the following days, should you ever return to your house to find your guests away, try locking them out. Park your car far away, lock the doors, and settle in for an extended home hibernation. When your guests return, stay away from all doors and windows. Don't answer the phone. Maintain total silence. You can pass the time sleeping, meditating, or reading in the closet.

Be careful. Like ducks fed bread crumbs by well-meaning humans, long-term guests may have become dependent on handouts. They may wait days or weeks in your driveway before tragically succumbing to deprivation and cold.

■ hardship

Though your guests may not accept hints or even statements suggesting they are putting you out, they are material beings and will respond to the physical conditions of their environment. Buy no food, cut off unnecessary services such as phone, cable, Internet, and electricity. Sell furniture. Turn off the heat. If your guests complain, explain that you're making sacrifices because of the "current situation."

Then wait them out. Eat all you can while at work or in the car. Buoy your spirits by imagining life without them and knowing that your glee can only be pissing them off.

DESPERATE MEASURES

Create a legal rationale for your guests' departure. Pretend to be your landlord and post your own eviction notice, specifically citing overoccupancy. Your moochers are unlikely to be aware of local zoning codes, so don't be concerned about the arbitrary or unfair nature of the notice. If necessary, fake phone calls to your lawyer, expressing outrage that your case, as reasonable as it is, is essentially unwinnable. As a last measure, pick a time when your guests will be away to throw their possessions *and your own* onto the street and "evict" yourself. Sob uncontrollably until they leave, banging on your own front door and blubbering about the wonderful memories forever locked inside.

7. encouraging someone who shouldn't be encouraged

You have a friend who's never quite accomplished anything. You've listened to her horrible ideas for so long that, when she mentions something slightly promising, you encourage her to do it, only because you don't want to be the perpetual bubble burster.

Of course, your encouragement has disastrous results. Empowered by your uncharacteristic enthusiasm, she quits her job, mortgages her house, and goes into business making cosmetics for dogs.

TACTICS

■ **poor execution**

Stand by your encouragement. The idea was great; the implementation was sloppy and mismanaged. Try to pin the blame on issues you weren't asked about: "The font on the lipstick is all wrong!" or "You went with *that* name?" or "Who told you to sell it in the bodega?"

■ **miscommunication**

Insist you misheard her plan, or she misheard your advice. If she opened a donut store, say you thought she said donut *storage*: "A donut store is a terrible idea. But I guess you found that out."

■ **rocky III**

Pretend her failure was part of a bigger plan: "I wanted you to see what it's like to have no material possessions. Now you're hungry. You've got nothing to lose. No house. No job. Zilch. Now go get 'em, tiger."

8. leaving a bad phone message

You hang up the phone, troubled. You've just left a message for someone you're trying to impress. Unfortunately, something weird happened. Something that will haunt you forever. Perhaps you called the
person—or his wife or child—the wrong name. Perhaps you revealed
inappropriate details about your own health or hygiene. Maybe you
stumbled in an embarrassing way, belched loudly, had your voice
break, or forgot your *own* name. Or perhaps you lost your temper,
yelling obscenities at the kids, at your wife, or at a supervisor.

You replay the message repeatedly in the answering machine of
your mind. You wonder who will be present when he plays it. His wife?
His children? A cynical friend? Will they be offended? Will they laugh?
Will they copy it and share it with coworkers, posting it on the Internet
for the comedy-starved masses?

TACTICS

■ you've heard it all before

Contact the person again through some alternate means. Call his cell phone, e-mail him, track him down at the golf course. When you finally reach him, give him a long-winded, boring version of the message you just left—leaving out, of course, the offending comments. Before you part, tell him you left the same message on his machine and that he can erase it.

■ signal-to-noise ratio

Call back and leave thirty brief messages explaining that your phone is on the fritz and you're "not sure if this is getting through." The hope is that, on returning home, the recipient sees a blinking 31 and feels the need to quickly skip through messages that aren't vital.

■ secret code

Call back and press your keypad frantically while his outgoing message is playing. If you happen to press the right code, you may be able to erase his messages remotely. Note: Most people who have attempted this have had no luck, even on their own machines with prior knowledge of the code.

9. feeling obligated to buy from a friend who makes crafts

One woman's art is another's junk. Why should you have to shell out a hundred and fifty bucks for some twine-and-soda-bottle wind chime? Just to maintain a friendship? Yes. Unless you can call upon one of the wallet-saving maneuvers below.

TACTICS

■ i can't decide

Rave about several of your friend's creations. Then focus in on two you're "just crazy about." But don't buy either. Deliberate. Mull them over. Ask for photos of each. Describe exactly where the object is going to go in your apartment. Ask for her opinion, but don't take it. Say you need to consult other friends, your husband, your decorator. Above all, leave. And don't come back to your friend's shop or home until she's abandoned this horrible sideline.

▪ tit for tat

As your friend will attest, one doesn't have to buy the things one makes oneself. So join the club. Create your own crappy knickknacks and show them off, or at least talk about them whenever she talks about hers. If she lays on the guilt by implying that hers are different from yours, barter with her so at least you don't have to lay out cash for her junk.

■ **"save it for the show"**

Pretend to fall in love with a piece. Expound about what a masterpiece it is, how artfully rendered, etc. But decline to purchase it, claiming it'll be best put to use in an upcoming exhibition at a gallery or museum. You're not refusing to buy it; you're refusing to shortchange her career by selfishly removing it from public circulation.

DESPERATE MEASURES

Once again, fall in love with a piece, but make sure it's small or has small parts. Claim that the presence of children in your household prevents your bringing home such a choking hazard. If you don't have children, worry about visiting nieces, nephews, or senile grandparents who "put everything in their mouths."

10. borrowing something and destroying it

If you're like most people, you break things you borrow more easily than things you own. It's not just that you're less familiar with devices you don't use frequently. It's also that you couldn't care less about other people's crap.

So when you run your neighbor's leaf blower with no oil, it's no surprise that the engine housing cracks to pieces on you. What is a surprise is exactly how much it costs to replace the damn thing, which you used for only twenty seconds for God's sake.

TACTICS

■ don't mention it

If the damage isn't apparent, return the item without mentioning the problem. It is possible that your neighbor won't use the leaf blower for months, by which time he'll have forgotten that you were the last

person to borrow it. If the damage is obvious, fix the cosmetic flaws cheaply (Krazy Glue, duct tape, a nail, etc.) and put it back in your neighbor's garage.

If the item is something your neighbor uses frequently, break an inexpensive but vital part and confess to the smaller sin. Insist on replacing the part yourself, but put off the repairs until leaf blowing season is over. When your neighbor next uses the twice-broken item, he might vaguely remember that you borrowed it last, but he will quite vividly remember your honesty and diligence in addressing the smaller problem, and chalk the larger problem up to normal wear and tear.

■ play offense

Grab the broken item and storm over to your neighbor's house in a rage. Scream at him about how irresponsible it was for him to let you borrow something so poorly maintained, or something about which you weren't properly instructed. Tell him you damn near killed yourself. Threaten to never borrow anything from him again.

■ wait it out

Over time, many items decrease in value. Wait long enough, and the item you borrowed and broke might go the way of memory chips, Japanese office space, recordable CDs, and Razor scooters. What's more, periods of general price deflation surface from time to time. A scythe borrowed and broken in 1929 could have been replaced for a third of the price in 1945, although by that time most people would have preferred a shiny new Ferguson Model 9 Grass-O-Matic.

11. purchasing embarrassing items

It's the moment you've been dreading. Your hemorrhoid gel is squeezed so flat you're not sure even a pair of scissors and a spatula would get you any more. Itchy but meek soul that you are, you decide to hit the drug store early Saturday morning when foot traffic is at a minimum. In fact, making the most of the empty checkout lines, you seize the moment to stock up on lice shampoo, fart pills, enemas, condoms, "Herpes Helper," and an internal massage wand.

Then, walking to the cashier, you bump into your childhood minister, who, eyes twinkling, greets you with a big, "Hello!" And notices your shopping cart of shame.

TACTICS

■ gag gift

Make no attempt to hide the contents of your cart. In fact, find an opportunity during the conversation to pull out a few items and laugh. "Can you believe this? Who really buys this stuff?" Explain that your friend is having a bachelorette party and you've been charged with assembling a silly gift basket of unsavories. It's not your idea of fun, but she has a strange sense of humor, and you want to be a good sport.

■ good samaritan

While you're chatting, grab other items that suggest you aren't shopping for yourself: a cane, a footbath, reading glasses, a hernia truss, adult diapers, or old people's vitamins. When your minister stares at one of these products for too long, mention that your great-grandmother has trouble getting to the store these days.

■ **burial**

Quickly toss anything you can into your cart, burying the offensive products beneath reams of notebooks, tuna cans, and inflatable pools. Even if he's already seen the embarrassing stuff, your minister may now surmise you have an obsessive shopping disorder or have begun part-time work as a destocking clerk.

12. being asked to recommend someone who is undeserving

Over lunch, a friend tells you she's applying for a job at CorpTech. "CorpTech?" you say, "That's Harold Berman's company! I work with him all the time!" You should have kept your mouth shut. Your friend begs you to write a letter of recommendation, an act whose refusal would leave a most awkward silence in its wake.

Making the task especially hard is the fact that your friend is a lazy, incompetent dilettante. Your Hobson's choice: Recommend her and risk losing respect and credibility, or write a nasty recommendation and risk that, hired or not, she learns of it.

TACTICS

■ sarcastic tone

Imbue your letter of recommendation with a sarcastic tone that belies the laudatory words on the page. The more effusive you appear, the stronger your real message will be. You might write, "She would be *so* amazing selling for you. There's no one who could *possibly* sell as well as she could. *God.*"

While your sarcasm might not be apparent to the potential employer, it provides cover should he come back to you wondering why you recommended a buffoon. Shoot back, "What are you talking about?" and grab the letter from his hands, reading it with the proper tone and emphasis. When finished, tell him that merely writing a negative recommendation wouldn't have cut it. You needed to be sarcastic to sufficiently convey the contempt you have for the applicant.

Of course, should your friend obtain a copy of the letter, she will be overjoyed and reminded of your undying loyalty and support.

▪ "i pissed berman off"

Sadly inform your friend that you've burned your bridges to Berman. Say, "We had a major falling out. I can still write the recommendation if you want me to, but I think it'll do more harm than good. Considering he hates my guts and all."

If, idiot that your friend is, she still wants you to pen the letter, forge an honest appraisal, brimming with harsh words. Should she come upon the letter, remind her, "He hates me. I thought if I wrote it that way he'd hire you just to spite me."

▪ the right—other—stuff

Enumerate all the great qualities your friend has. Since none of these has any bearing on the job at hand, you'll neither support her candidacy nor earn her enmity. You might mention skills like crocheting, kayaking, and gardening. Or traits such as sound sleeping, hawk-like vision, and normal-to-oily hair. End your letter with the words, "For these reasons, as well as her second place finish in the sixth grade student council presidential election, I heartily recommend my friend for the open position."

WHILE WE OFTEN PREFER to think of others as the cause of our awkward moments, most of us realize that the problem lies deep within ourselves. In the next chapter, it's all coming out.

6 what's a body to do?

PRIVATE FUNCTIONS IN A PUBLIC WORLD

ELEANOR ROOSEVELT ONCE SAID, "No one can make you feel inferior without your consent."

Mrs. Roosevelt was wrong. The reason for her mistake lies within us. Literally. There are many activities our bodies perform *without our consent* that are—by any objective standard—inferior, humiliating, and awful.

In fact, it's precisely because these activities occur without our consent that they are a problem. If we could choose the time and place to run out of toilet paper, fart, or sport wood, most of us would feel far less inferior.

But there is hope. Even when our bodies betray us, our minds can guide us to corrective action. If we prepare.

1. finding a bathroom

Nature often calls when facilities are scarce. Typically, you're walking through an unfamiliar area, having maxed out your bladder in the expectation of reaching your destination soon. You scan the landscape frantically, the physical pressure and rising blood toxin levels clouding your brain and making your search that much more difficult.

TACTICS

■ hotels

There is no brighter beacon in your time of need than the patron saint of toilet seekers, the hotel.

There are, however, several guidelines to keep in mind to avoid detection and removal by unsympathetic clerks. Remember: A screw-up now is serious. As you entered the hotel lobby, your body, anticipating sweet relief, moved into stage four of its excretory function: the final-countdown. Should you encounter further delay, your body is liable to become frustrated with your mind and take matters into its own hands.

Stride confidently past the front desk as if you know precisely where you're going. Do not stop and look for signs or ask an employee. Just march to a promising hallway and look for a bathroom. If none is to be found, march right back with the same purposeful look and head to another likely passage. This process will eventually lead you to salvation.

If you have a choice of hotels, choose a high-end corporate chain. Its bathrooms will be clean and well equipped, and its employees less likely to offend possible guests by questioning suspicious persons with strained expressions.

■ small restaurants

Large restaurants and fast food establishments are easy prey for the committed urinator/defecator. But what of the smaller, more "boutique-y" restaurants? Those that, for reasons of limited space and romantic atmosphere, often post preemptive signs stating REST ROOMS FOR PATRONS ONLY?

In a pinch, even these vigilant fortresses can be breached with proper technique. If the eatery has a bar, and you're willing to drop a few bucks, order a soda and head to the bathroom while your glass is being filled. If there's no bar, or if your budget's as tight as your sphincter, ask the maître d' for a menu. As you read it, nod agreeably and, like a Ouija board planchette, drift toward the bathroom. After emerging, lighter and happier, hand the menu back, saying, "This looks great," and ask if they'd set aside a table for a party of seven. Whatever the host's response, say thank you and depart.

■ **open houses**

Especially useful on Sundays when many restaurants are closed, the open house affords you an at-home experience on the road.

Walk into the condo, house, or apartment and, if required, sign in with a false name. Establish credibility by grabbing all the literature you can and asking a purchase-ready question such as, "What's the soonest I could move in?" Begin your tour and, if the realtor follows you, insist on exploring alone to "get a better feel for things." When you find an empty bathroom, your tour is over. Note: If the dwelling is newly constructed, run the tap to make sure there's water. Lack of water needn't stop you, but should certainly hasten your exit.

■ **construction sites**

While not the most elegant facilities, those found at construction sites are often the most accessible. For added insurance, take a few simple steps to look like you belong.

First, clip your cell phone to your belt. If you're wearing an undershirt, remove all layers above it. Finally, do something constructive: Stack a few pieces of plywood, inspect an electrical panel, or pace out distances in the yard, counting loudly.

After emerging from the Porta-John, complain to an imaginary contractor on your cell phone: "Why'd you send me out here? Everything's fine. Except the Porta-Potty—but I think that's 'cause non-workers are using it."

street smarts

Once in a while, none of the above opportunities presents itself. Even when "roughing it," it's worth taking a moment to pick the best spot. Look for an area where your actions will be in harmony with the surroundings: a stand of wild ficus, a thicket of oak, or a back-alley Dumpster. Pay attention to the acoustic properties of the surface you threaten. Strive for highly damped materials, such as weeds, hay, or fresh snow. Avoid acoustically reflective substances such as dried leaves, liquids, and sheet metal.

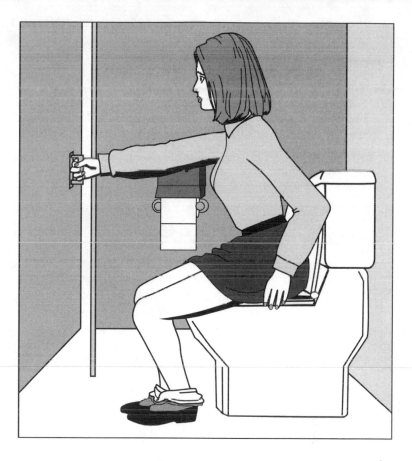

2. using a lockless bathroom

Nothing expresses disdain for guests more than a lockless bathroom. It puts the unsuspecting visitor in embarrassment's path, with disaster a mere doorknob twist away. Luckily, the options for recourse are simple, easy to remember, and surprisingly effective.

TACTICS

■ knee brace

If the toilet is close to the bathroom entrance, sit on the seat (regardless of your sex or purpose) and use your tibia and fibula as diagonal crossbraces, keeping your knee pressed firmly against the center of the door. DO NOT LOCK THE KNEE. By allowing some give when the door is pushed, you alert others too rude to knock to the fact that a human being and not an errant wastebasket is obstructing the door.

■ rattlesnake

Loudly clear your throat, whistle a tune, or rustle a newspaper. Like a rattlesnake, increase the volume as footsteps approach, gently sending the message, "I am here, and I will not look favorably upon trespassers."

■ the wedge

Jam a thick rug, rubberized bath mat, or shoe under the door, creating a wedge, nature's simplest machine. This will turn the intruder's own energy against him, redirecting it to the purpose of keeping the door fixed in space.

3. using a bathroom where noise carries

While the square footage and bedroom count of the average American home have increased over the past century, the quality of its construction has, sadly, declined. Mirroring modern society's obsession with image over substance, today's homes may boast six thousand square feet and six bedrooms, yet fail to match the workmanship of even the tiniest 1930s bungalow.

Nowhere is this more evident than in the bathroom door. Once the pride of the American abode, a rock-solid redoubt of old-growth oak, the bathroom door has become a pathetic pastiche of balsa wood, glue, and cardboard chunks, topped off like a clown's nose with a made-in-China alloy knob.

Gone are the days when the master of the house, waistcoat busting with beans, pork chops, and rutabagas, could confidently close the bathroom door and do his business with no fear of disturbing his wife's friends knitting across the hall.

Today, he cowers in the bathroom, aware that everyone else in the house might as well be perched on the sink beside him listening to his every pop, whistle, and squeak. Worse, he takes false comfort in the overhead fan, deluding himself into thinking its high-pitched whirr will somehow overcome the distinctly low-register explosions emanating from his innards.

TACTICS

■ distance makes the fart grow softer

As everyone knows, sound's amplitude decreases with the square of the distance. Time your lavatory visits to coincide with events that pull people far away, such as the unveiling of a humorous lawn ornament, the opening of presents on the patio, or a dramatic game of horseshoes. If no such distractions are likely to transpire, manufacture your own. Mention the rare blue rings visible around Venus this week, or ask if anyone else has noticed the tall blonde undressing in the window across the street. Then hit the can, pronto

■ **partner up**

Find a kindred spirit and take turns covering for each other by making patently silly sounds to obscure those coming from the bathroom while the other is in it. Especially effective are raspberries, Bronx cheers, and "armpit farts" that paint their authentic counterparts with the brush of phoniness.

■ **patience**

The much loved "squeaky voice" party trick that results from inhaling helium does not in any way rely on a physiological change of the vocal chords. Rather, it speeds the flow of air through the larynx, effectively raising the pitch and volume of your voice.

Slowing down the flow of air through other passages in the body can have a similar muting effect. So relax, take your time, and strive for a pitch more familiar to mating humpbacks than people.

4. hiding an erection

If you're a typical adult male, you think about sex every ten seconds. Even if only one percent of these thoughts are spicy enough to produce an erection, you're looking at eighty-six woodies a day.

Perhaps a few of these puppies will be well timed to private or semiprivate moments. That still leaves you scrambling to contain dozens upon dozens of embarrassing flare-ups. And, sometimes, the very act of containment can draw attention to an otherwise unnoticed tentpole.

TACTICS

■ the shield

In ancient times, centurions used their shields both to stave off attacks and to maintain their honor while guarding the vestal virgins in the Forum Romanum.

While you are unlikely to carry around a thirty-pound iron plate, perhaps you have a bag of groceries or a briefcase handy that can be used in a similar way. To explain your front-and-center carrying style, lean back and breathe effortfully, as if the heavy weight of your load requires a pose normally restricted to Scottish caber tossers.

■ magician

Draw attention away from your groin by excitedly waving something eye-catching in the air: a handkerchief, a lottery ticket, a trophy. Keep your hand in motion to create an air of mystery. Maintain laserlike focus on the object, since confused passersby will be looking to you for guidance.

■ layering

Many garments can be used to break up your silhouette and create a rumpled look. Experiment with whatever you're wearing but mix, match, and layer in exciting new ways. Untuck shirttails, tie a jacket around your waist, or stretch a baggy sweatshirt into a kilt. Fashion is about having fun.

■ please be seated

If you're standing, sit down. If you're seated, don't get up. Say your leg fell asleep, there's a rock in your shoe, or your heart stopped. While seated, you can work the erection into a less conspicuous position by crossing and uncrossing your legs. Or you can simply wait it out.

baseball and dead kittens

Any of the preceding techniques can be enhanced by calling forth nonsexual imagery to compete with the prurient pictures flipping through your mind. This is a personal choice. For some, thoughts of baseball acromegalic Randy Johnson will quickly shrivel even the most turgid erection. Others, of course, find the Big Unit's mulleted, chinless face wildly erotic, engorging their member to the point of pain and beyond.

■ **time for your close-up**

If you are near a wall, stand within a few inches of it and pretend to examine its surface in extreme detail. This works well in art museums or galleries where only an extremely close look reveals the artist's technique. What's more, if an especially racy work of art has *caused* the problem, getting a closer look will turn lusty bodies into abstract dabs of paint and grains of silver halide.

5. clogging someone else's toilet

You have been invited to dine at the home of a friend. You arrive, face painted, hair coiffed, body sheathed in colorful fabrics. You partake in thoughtful discussions of matters cultural, political, and scientific. The meal, too, is splendid: fine wines, choice meats, sumptuous desserts. You feel like a princess, marveling in the splendor of your existence. You excuse yourself to use the lavatory.

And then you clog the toilet. Suddenly you are not a princess. You are a naughty monkey who has escaped from the zoo and damaged a human being's property in a most repulsive way. For the moment, only you know you are a monkey. But, unless you act fast, it will soon become apparent to all.

TACTICS

■ the discoverer

If you've been quick, pretend you have not yet used the bathroom. Stand at the threshold, like Balboa at the Pacific, and point to your "discovery," discreetly saying, "Someone appears to have had a problem."

■ systemic failure

Quickly visit every other bathroom in the house and fill the toilets with tissue until none will flush. Then return to your hostess and say you've checked every bathroom and there seems to be some sort of systemic problem. Blame the sewer or septic system.

■ occupado

If you can, lock the door behind you. If not, lock it from inside and jump out a window. The hosts and the other guests will assume someone else is inside. By the time the hosts discover the real problem, they will be unable to pin the blame on you.

6. farting around others

The only thing worse than thinking you lack privacy is thinking you have privacy when you don't.

This applies to so many activities, from sniffing your armpits to downloading porn, from picking your nose to scratching your ass. Fortunately, with some foresight and a creaky door, you will usually have sufficient warning when others approach.

Not so with the fart. A fart emitted thoughtfully in total seclusion can be a source of embarrassment even several minutes later. Unless you take action.

TACTICS

■ **open window policy**

By keeping the windows of your office open, you not only help dissipate the stench, you also have a built-in excuse should someone arrive during a "regional air-quality alert." After the unwelcome visitor has entered, walk to a window and make a big show of shutting it, muttering about the "horrible stink out there." If possible, blame a nearby paper mill, sewage treatment plant, or sausage cart.

■ **hvac**

Complain to your guest about the ductwork around your office. "I thought this was a great office when I picked it, but I'd forgotten that the vents come straight up from Johnson's office. I sure wish that guy would lay off the Mexican food!"

hear no evil

If you've had success with the previous techniques, you might be tempted to "push the envelope" by farting in front of others. Be careful. Even when the air inside you screams "silent," the fart can scream, "Brrrrrrrrrrrt!" Avoid such nasty surprises by covering your farts with other sounds. Shift your body in a notoriously squeaky leather chair. Pop plastic packing bubbles by the fistful. Or cough loudly at precisely the right moment. (Although, in the last case, realize that you're at risk of visitors thinking you have monstrously bad breath.)

7. running out of toilet paper

Maybe you're the trusting sort. Maybe you began your task in a distracted state of high crisis. Or maybe you're the Chuck Yeager type, the hardcore thrill seeker who ignores low fuel lights on lonely desert highways. Whatever the reason, you're stuck with your pants down. You've done your business and don't have the material to professionally finish the job.

TACTICS

▪ strength in numbers

If there is more than one stall in the bathroom, you're in luck. Check to see if there's someone next to you. If so, knock and ask for paper. Get right to the point. If you begin your query with "Pssst . . ." or "Hey, buddy . . ." he might mistake the overture for an entirely different type of inter-stall activity. If alone, reach under the wall to fish for the leading edge of the paper roll. Pull it slowly until you've gathered enough to complete the job.

▪ substitution

If the bathroom's a single-seater, it's time to think outside the stall. Take inventory of everything in the room. Rank the items based on softness, strength, and flushability. Tissues beat towels. Towels beat socks. Socks beat curtains. Everything beats razor blades.

▪ you be stylin'

Go baggy. Pull your pants at least six inches below the navel to create a buffer space between your skin and clothing. Then shuffle out, making a "Yo!" gesture and strutting your badass self to a supply closet or another bathroom to finish the job.

IN THE PREVIOUS SITUATIONS, your embarrassment was forged by a common perspective with the people around you. What about situations with no cultural norms? No common language? No rules? How do you get yourself out of a mess when you don't even know what you did wrong?

7 clash of civilizations:

STAYING ON THE GOOD SIDE OF 6.3 BILLION PEOPLE

IN CHINA, IT'S CONSIDERED horrible manners to stifle a burp. In Guatemala, one can draw the locals' ire by unpeeling more than half a banana at any one time. And closer to home, in Canada, playing doubles tennis with four people is considered a contemptible bastardization of the sport of kings.

Nothing is more difficult than avoiding awkwardness when you're with others who don't share your customs. Moreover, awkwardness may not be the only consequence. Committing a cultural gaffe may lead not merely to ridicule or social isolation, but to a painful and untimely death.

1. ordering off a foreign cuisine menu

You've managed to snag a date with the attractive stewardess from across the hall. You'd gotten no response for months, but then she glimpsed the Antonioni video that you mistakenly thought had nude scenes and she asked if you'd ever been to Italy. Desperate, you smiled broadly and rattled off a bunch of villages you know only from the Little Caesar's placemat.

Now the two of you are sitting in an authentic northern Italian restaurant. So authentic, in fact, you can't make out the menu. You scan the dishes nervously, afraid of mispronouncing even the simplest one or, worse, nailing it only to learn you've ordered dolphin testicles in spleen sauce.

TACTICS

▪ nickname

Scour the menu for a single word you can pronounce. When ordering, use that word to indicate the entire dish from whose description it comes. Strive for a casual, affectionate tone, as if this is your shorthand for a dish you've enjoyed many, many times in the old country. Make sure the word is unique to the item. For example, simply saying "marinara" could refer to more than half the items on the menu.

▪ "stop right there"

As your waiter describes the specials, fill his pauses with approving nods, grunts, and mouth-watering gulps. When his voice rises to complete a description, hold up your hand and say, "Stop right there. That's what I want. Bring it to me. Now."

■ a picture is worth a thousand foreign words

Don't open the menu. Watch the wait staff carry dishes to nearby patrons. When you see something that looks palatable, grab that waiter, telling him, "That's what I want. That. That looks perfect." If he tries to explain what it is, interrupt him, saying, "I know what it is. I've just never seen it done so well. Bring it to me. Now."

■ staff pick

Being a waiter at an exclusive restaurant isn't just a job; it's a profession. Thus, it's considered not only appropriate but quite sophisticated to ask your waiter to select your meal. In fact, by so doing you may impress your date even more than by an accurate pronunciation of "vongoline di aranciata trapanette a due eliche."

If your waiter brings out dolphin in spleen sauce, refer to earlier sections of this book relating to discreet disposal of horrible food.

2. reaching the limits
of your foreign language skills

A little knowledge is a dangerous thing. When it comes to foreign language skills, it can be downright deadly.

First, attempts to impress others with a smattering of well-pronounced phrases may lead native speakers to rattle off a long and hard-to-follow torrent of words for which you have no response other than to stare blankly, a thread of drool falling from the corner of your gaping mouth.

Worse, you might emphatically state something you don't mean at all—something preposterous or insulting or utterly inappropriate. This problem frequently arises when words closely resemble innocuous conversational tidbits you meant to offer. For example, rather than saying "Adelante!" ("Come in") to an elderly stranger, you might shout, "Andale! Andale!"—a phrase more closely associated with cartoon stereotype Speedy Gonzalez.

TACTICS

■ focused vocabulary work

Learn every form of apology, from "I regret my error" to "I am eternally rueful I have misled you into thinking I know anything of your exquisite language. I am a buffoon."

■ "I'm not dumb. i'm deaf"

Start tapping your ear, the international symbol meaning, "I'm deaf." The insulted party will understand, if not excuse, your rude outbursts.

DESPERATE MEASURES

Continue uttering statements of varied offensiveness, but in a spastic and involuntary manner. The insulted foreigner will be overjoyed at the opportunity to tell friends and family he was nonjudgmental and accepting of a person with Tourette's.

3. having problems telling two people apart

While politically incorrect to mention, the fact remains: It's hard to distinguish between people who don't look like you. Our visual recognition skills were honed when we lived in small, genetically similar tribes. Because of this, the modern-day brain is not prepared to make fine differentiations within racial groups—an awkward truth in a world where Melanesians, Inuits, and Bushmen may all be riding the same subway car.

Unfortunately, when you meet your Korean pals Steve and Joe for a drink and accidentally call them Joe and Steve, don't expect some paperback bastardization of Darwinian theory to ease their pain.

TACTICS

■ data fitting

Insist that your confusion is solely the result of one of the countless other things they have in common. Maybe Steve and Joe both play baseball. Or enjoy rock candy. Or buy super premium unleaded.

Seize on these meager points of commonality and insist they're the source of your confusion. If your friends are dubious, bring up charges of reverse racism: "Oh, I guess all Asians look the same to us white guys! White guys are so stupid! Don't ask a white guy to tell people apart!"

■ doppelgänger

If only one person is present, insist the mistake is not connected with the other person they know. Say, "There's a second Steve who's your twin, I swear. He's not even Asian! He's Latino! But he's you! It's friggin' weird, man. It's some kind of doppelgänger."

■ cockeye

Fail to acknowledge your mistake and proceed to make a variety of similar visual errors—looking at one thing while calling it something else. For example, stare at the wall and say, "Hey, look what's on TV!" Eventually, you should be able to convince your friends you're cockeyed. When they're puzzled by its sudden onset, say you must have failed to take your prescription that morning. "I thought I grabbed the cockeye pills. It must have been the Tic Tacs. Typical cockeye move."

4. participating in
unfamiliar ceremonies

Nothing is more terrifying than partaking in an unfamiliar cultural or religious ceremony. Not only are the language and rituals strange, but a strict schedule of alternating chants and silence makes it impossible to ask questions.

Moreover, everyone's so damned serious, whether they're throwing wood chips, eating tiny wafers, dancing with a pig, or washing an old man's feet. And there's the nagging feeling your role will be something akin to Jessica Lange's in the ape appeasement scene from *King Kong*.

So when the invitation arrives for the Zoroastrian coming-of-age ceremony for your herbalist's daughter, read on so you don't get tossed in the volcano.

TACTICS

■ a splendid guest

Don't be first. Don't be last. Move slowly. Move late. Don't eat anything unless others insist and make sure your bite is small enough so everyone else can enjoy a similar size portion. Stay calm. Imagine you are home watching all this on *National Geographic Explorer*.

■ **monkey see, monkey do**

Search the crowd for someone resembling you in sex, age, and appearance. Do exactly what he does. If he stands, stand. If he sings, mumble along. If he self-flagellates with a myrtle branch, grab a switch and join the fun.

If possible, select a mentor who seems knowledgeable but apathetic—a sullen teenager or a fat guy with indigestion—someone doing no more than necessary to avoid disapproving glares and angry elbows in his side.

■ **giggle control**

If you feel a laugh coming on, bite your lip or stomp on your toe. If neither approach works, give in to the laughter, raising your arms to the skies in grateful rapture, or rolling ecstatically on the floor like a Holy Spirit–powered jumping bean.

5. determining if others are speaking english

At the airport, a stranger asks you a question. Although he speaks loudly and confidently, you don't understand a word. Perhaps he's from Central Asia and, seeing the polyester sweatsuit you threw on this morning, assumes that you are too. Or perhaps he's speaking English but in a way that you don't recognize. He might have a speech impediment or a heavy accent or an incompetent night school instructor.

But you can't simply ask, "Are you speaking English?"

If an industrious foreigner has made an effort to learn English, a language with 431 irregular verbs and 18,357 idioms, he is sure to be insulted by your suggestion that his efforts are for naught.

A native English speaker will be even more insulted, since you're implying that his regional dialect or pronunciation is so inferior as to render unrecognizable even a single building block of the English language, like "and," "of," "the," or "hamburger."

TACTICS

■ go nonnative

Pretend *you're* a foreigner and, in a thick, untraceable accent, ask if your questioner would "pleased to speak more slowly." Strain to explain that English is not your first language and comes only with great difficulty. Real foreigners will leave you alone. English speakers will repeat their query loudly and slowly, giving you a decent shot at responding to them and satisfying your curiosity about their origins.

■ scotland

Excitedly say, "You must be from Scotland!" If they are, they'll be thrilled. If not, Scotland is an innocuous enough place that no one is likely to take great offense. There are also a few weird Gaelic languages up there, so non-English speakers won't feel totally excluded. Either way, they'll leave you alone or clue you in to exactly which accent you're dealing with.

■ ill at ease

Tap into the natural discomfort you're feeling but take it up a notch, acting mentally disturbed, challenged, or outer spacey. The questioner will quickly move on to a normal human and try again.

afterword

You've done it. Assuming you didn't skip ahead, you are now immune to the effects of your own rudeness, stupidity, and insensitivity.

Think you're ready to face the slings and arrows of outrageous awkwardness? Think again. You have one more lesson to master:

HIDE THIS BOOK.

Put it in a safe place, like the bottom of your sock drawer, and lock the doors and draw the blinds when referencing it.

We'd like to ask you to recommend this book to friends. But we can't. That request is completely at odds with our greater mission: protecting you, gentle reader, from the ill effects of awkwardness. After all, nothing would be more embarrassing than showing off the new, more confident you only to have some jealous friend trace it to a flimsy paperback.

So let's keep it our little secret. And if some day you reach a position of importance—say, U. S. senator or Wall Street millionaire—you might remember to thank those who got you there.

about the authors

Gregg Kavet and Andy Robin have written for film and television, including *Saturday Night Live* and *Seinfeld,* where their scripts centered on such awkward moments as forgetting a girlfriend's name and switching barbers. They were nominated for three Emmys, and their script "The Fatigues" won the 1997 Writers Guild Award for outstanding comedy. This is their first book.